An Introductory Economics Workbook

Second Edition

G. F. Stanlake MA BSc (Econ)

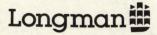

Also by G F Stanlake

First Economics
Introductory Economics
Macroeconomics: an Introduction
A Macroeconomics Workbook (with B Harrison)
Objective Tests in Economics
Public Finance (*Longman Economic Studies* series)

LONGMAN GROUP UK LIMITED
*Longman House, Burnt Mill, Harlow, Essex CM20 2JE, England
and Associated Companies throughout the World*

First published 1980
Second edition 1985
Second impression 1987

ISBN 0 582 35484 6

Produced by Longman Singapore Publishers Pte Ltd
Printed in Singapore

Preface

Although this workbook was originally written as a complementary text to *Introductory Economics*, the summaries, the sequence of topics, the variety and level of the questions and the detailed nature of many of the answers, will make it eminently suitable for use as an independent aid to students on any Economics course at approximately A-level standard.

It is not simply a book of questions. The text contains summaries of the main topics and many of the answers are developed at some length.

It is hoped that the inclusion of several different types of question (short answer, multiple choice, true/false and data response) will add interest to the exercises. To this end I have also tried to vary, as much as possible, the type of material on which the exercises are based. There are questions based on quotations, graphs, arithmetical exercises, current statistics and material culled from periodicals.

I have tried, I hope with success, to strike a balance which is both instructive and stimulating between questions which probe the understanding of economic theory and questions which test the abilities to see the relevance of that theory and to use it in making sense of contemporary economic problems.

I must acknowledge with gratitude the considerable help I have received from Mr B. Harrison.

G F Stanlake

Acknowledgement

We are grateful to the following for permission to reproduce photographs on the cover:

Homer Sykes (left);   Ray Green (centre);   Keystone/CLI (right).

Contents

Answers

Questions

Part 1

The nature, scope and methods of economics

Introduction

The fundamental feature of economic life is that people find themselves in a situation of scarcity and, hence, are forced to make choices. Technical and scientific progress has led to enormous increases in output per head during the present century, but peoples' appetites for material satisfactions have also increased and more than kept pace with the growth in productivity.

In all societies people want more than they are capable of producing. At any given moment in time the supply of economic resources is limited so that more of one thing can be produced only if less of something else is produced. Likewise incomes are limited and in spending our incomes we have to choose between alternatives. Economists use the term *opportunity cost* to describe the idea of measuring cost in terms of the alternatives foregone.

Faced with the problem of unlimited wants and limited means of satisfying these wants, all societies have to make decisions on resource allocation, that is, how to deploy the limited resources so as to maximise economic welfare. The basic economic problems facing all societies are

(a) *what* goods and services to produce,
(b) *how* these goods and services should be produced,
(c) *for whom* these goods and services should be produced.

The first two questions represent problems of production while (c) is a problem of distribution.

In traditional societies where the way of life has remained unchanged for hundreds or perhaps thousands of years these economic problems are solved by ancient custom. The traditional methods of production and distribution are faithfully followed by each generation.

One way in which the economic problems may be dealt with is for the state to take over ownership and control of economic resources. It can then allocate these resources and control production according to some national plan (which will also determine the distribution of the national output). This type of economic system is described as a command economy or centrally planned economy.

An alternative way of dealing with the problem of resource allocation is for the state to play a very minor role and for the market forces of demand and supply acting through the price mechanism to determine the nature of the output, the methods of production and the distribution of the national output.

This type of economy is known as a market or capitalist economy, a major feature of which is the private ownership of land and capital. In a market economy a person's willingness and ability to pay the price is the major determinant of the quantities and variety of the different goods and services produced.

Most societies contain some elements of all three types of economic system but in the modern world there is a clear distinction between countries which have adopted a socialist or communist system where centralised planning and public ownership of resources predominate, and mixed economies where the state has an important influence on economic activity but where the operation of market forces and the price mechanism are allowed to play a major part in the allocation of resources. Private ownership of land and capital is an important feature of mixed economies but not of centrally planned economies.

Economics is regarded as a science because economists use scientific method to develop and test their theories. Hypotheses which attempt to explain how one thing (e.g. price) is related to another (e.g. supply) are formulated on the basis of assumptions or, more likely, on the basis of observed behaviour. These hypotheses (e.g. 'a higher price will call forth a greater supply') are then tested to see if they fit the facts of economic life. If such a hypothesis is supported by factual evidence it is then framed as an economic 'law' or theory. A successful theory is one which can be used with a high degree of reliability to predict the outcome of certain events. When facts emerge which refute the theory it must be discarded and a search undertaken for a more satisfactory theory.

Since economics deals with human behaviour, economists cannot test their theories in laboratory experiments; they can only be tested against events as they unfold. The fact that the behaviour of any one individual is highly unpredictable does not invalidate the formulation of economic theories because the subject is concerned with the behaviour of large groups (e.g. the workers in an industry, the consumers of a particular product, or the members of a trade union). It is possible to make successful predictions about the behaviour of large groups. While there is always some degree of disagreement between economists on the merits of alternative theories (and new and unproven theories are always emerging), the major disputes arise on questions of economic policy. This is understandable because while a fair measure of agreement is likely to be achieved on questions of *how* the economic system works, it is highly probable that the question of *how it should* work will lead to controversy.

Short answer questions

1 A well-known definition of economics reads as follows
  'Economics is a science which studies human behaviour as a relation between ends and scarce means which have alternative uses.'
  a What are the *scarce means* referred to in the above statement?

b Which part of the definition makes reference to the idea of opportunity cost?

2 Visitors to developed countries from low-income countries often remark on the apparent abundance of all kinds of consumer goods in the shops and in people's homes. In what sense, therefore, can these goods be described as scarce?

3 The concept of opportunity cost can be effectively illustrated by making use of a production *possibility* curve. Explain the relevance of the word in italics.

4 When used in a commercial sense, the word *distribution* normally refers to activities such as wholesaling and retailing. To what activities does the word refer when it is used in economic analysis?

5 Explain how *the price mechanism* functions to reallocate resources in the following cases.
a An unexpectedly bad harvest causes the price of potatoes to be much higher than farmers had expected.
b Technical progress dramatically reduces the costs of producing electricity.
c The demand for tea falls as the public display an increasing preference for coffee.
d The development of video cassette recorders makes it possible for people to use their television sets to watch films of their own choice in the comfort of their own homes.

6 Economic systems are broadly classified into command economies (centrally planned economies), market economies, and traditional economies. In which type of economy are the following features most likely to be found?
a Economic resources are allocated by a system of licences and permits and not according to people's ability to pay market prices.
b Profits and losses are the main indicators of economic efficiency.
c The prices of many goods and services are not determined by the current demand and supply conditions but are administered (i.e. fixed by public authority).
d Most of the capital used in industry and commerce is owned by numerous shareholders.

7 Collective goods (or public goods) are those whose consumption cannot be confined to the individuals who are willing to pay for them.
a Give some examples of collective goods and services.
b Name one other feature of collective goods and services in addition to the one given in the above definition.

8 During the present century, governments in mixed economies have tended to play an increasing part in controlling and influencing economic activity. Give some examples of the manner in which governments intervene in the private sector to

a raise or lower market prices,
b influence the level of exports and imports,
c control the size of firms,
d influence the location of industry.

9 A major reason for government intervention is the existence of *externalities*. These consist of social costs and social benefits which are not taken account of in free market prices. Identify some possible externalities in the following situations.

a A dam constructed for irrigation purposes.
b Several residents in a particular road spend substantial sums of money on improving the external appearances of their houses.
c The conversion of coal-fired pottery kilns (i.e. ovens) to gas or electricity.
d The replacement of overhead electricity and telephone cables by underground lines.
e The construction of a by-pass around a busy market town.

10 Economists, when using scientific method, deal with what *is* rather than with what *ought to be*. In other words they make *positive* rather than *normative* statements. Which of the following are positive statements and which are normative?

a Unemployment has risen substantially during the past five years.
b The consumption of alcohol should be restricted by means of higher taxes on the commodity.
c Private ownership of the means of production is not in the public interest.
d The government should reduce the rate of income tax in order to increase the incentive to work.
e Increases in output per head can be used as indicators of economic progress.

11 'It is never possible to prove the validity of any theory in economics with 100 per cent certainty.' Why is this a true statement?

12 Unlike the physicist or chemist, the economist cannot test the validity of his theories by laboratory experiment. How, then, can economic theories be tested?

Multiple choice questions

13 The basic economic problem common to all societies is

A   the elimination of inflation.
B   the achievement of full employment.
C   what, how and for whom to produce.
D   the achievement of a satisfactory balance of payments position.

14

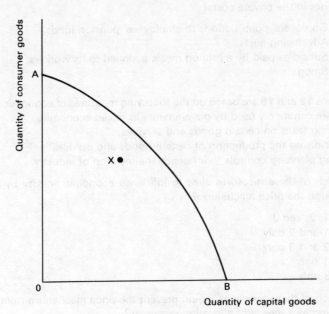

Figure 1

In Figure 1, AB is the community's production possibility curve. The point X represents

A   a combination of capital and consumer goods which is not attainable.
B   an output which can only be achieved at the cost of inflation.
C   a less than full employment output.
D   an optimum combination of capital and consumer goods.

15 Opportunity cost refers to

A   the revenue or earnings foregone as a result of a missed opportunity.
B   additional expenditure incurred as a result of failing to anticipate a rise in prices.
C   the capital losses suffered by shareholders when they fail to foresee a fall in share prices.
D   the sacrifice of the next most desired alternative.

16 Which of the following could *not* be provided in a competitive market?

A   Postal services.
B   Education services.
C   The services provided by lighthouses.
D   Hospital services.

17 Which of the following would be included in the social costs of production but not in the private costs?

A   Employers' contributions to employees' pension funds.
B   Advertising costs.
C   Subsidies paid by a firm on meals supplied to its workers.
D   Smog.

Questions **18** and **19** are based on the following measures of economic policy which are commonly used by governments in mixed economies.
1   Placing taxes on certain goods and services.
2   Subsidising the production of certain goods and services.
3   Using planning controls to influence the location of industry.

18 Which of these measures aims to influence economic activity by acting through the price mechanism?

A   1, 2, and 3
B   1 and 2 only
C   2 and 3 only
D   1 only
E   3 only

19 Which of these measures would prevent the price mechanism from functioning as a means of allocating resources?

A   1, 2, and 3
B   1 and 2 only
C   2 and 3 only
D   1 only
E   3 only

20 The question is based on the following economic features.
1   A method of rationing exists which is based almost completely on prices
2   There is a very large measure of consumer sovereignty
3   Income is derived from the ownership of property as well as from the sale of labour services.

Which of the above is (are) features of a market economy?

A   1, 2, and 3
B   1 and 2 only
C   2 and 3 only
D   1 only
E   3 only

True or false?

21 a The problem of scarcity may be overcome by increasing everyone's money income.

b There is no such thing as a free lunch.

c The fact that people in Western Europe now have a very much higher standard of living than they had fifty years ago disproves the notion that scarcity is a common and continuing feature of all societies.

d The price mechanism allocates resources to those who can afford to pay the market price.

e Economists usually agree on matters of economic policy but rarely agree on questions of economic analysis.

f A mixed economy is characterised by the absence of any public ownership of resources.

g The concept of opportunity cost is only relevant when resources have alternative uses.

Data response question

22 A society has a labour force of twelve men all equally competent and all capable of producing either commodity X or commodity Y. All other resources are specific to the production of one commodity. The potential outputs of each product are as follows.

Commodity X		Commodity Y	
Number of men	Weekly output (units)	Number of men	Weekly output (units)
1	10	1	50
2	20	2	80
3	30	3	100
4	40	4	120
5	50	5	136
6	60	6	150
7	70	7	162
8	80	8	172
9	90	9	181
10	100	10	189
11	110	11	196
12	120	12	200

a Draw the production possibility curve for this community.

b Is labour productivity higher in the industry producing commodity Y than in the industry producing commodity X?

Give reasons for your answer.

c What is the opportunity cost of producing 10 more units of X when the current output of Y is 120 units?

d The shape of the production possibility curve indicates that the cost of Y in terms of X_____ as the production of Y increases. What is the missing word?

Part 2

The factors of production

Introduction

In economics, the term *production* includes all those activities which contribute towards the satisfaction of material wants and for which people are prepared to pay a price. The output resulting from productive activities may be conveniently classified into non-durable consumer goods, durable consumer goods, producer goods (or capital), and services. Likewise the processes of production may be subdivided into three broad categories: extractive industries, manufacturing (or process) industries, and service industries.

The economic resources used in production are commonly described as *factors of production* and are divided into three main types: natural resources, human resources, and man-made resources. More generally they are described as *land, labour* and *capital*. Many economists include a fourth factor which is usually identified as *entrepreneurship* (organisation and risk-bearing).

A feature of modern production methods is the extent to which they make use of the principle of the *division of labour*. In many industries the principle has been applied to an extent which requires a very high degree of *specialisation* of labour and capital. These mass-production techniques, however, can only be utilised profitably where there is a large market for a standardised product.

Economists are always trying to improve their understanding of the things which determine

(*a*) the supply of and efficiency of the factors of production,
(*b*) the mobility of these factors (both occupationally and geographically),
(*c*) the ways in which the factors of production are combined and organised into productive units.

In economic analysis an important distinction is made between short-run and long-run changes in production. *In the short-run*, some of the factors employed by a firm (e.g. buildings and machinery) are fixed in supply, and changes in output can only be achieved by using more or less of the variable factors (e.g. labour and materials). *In the long-run*, the firm is able to change the *scale* of its production (i.e. to vary the quantities of all the factors employed).

In the short-run, as more of a variable factor is employed, output will increase more-than-proportionately, proportionately, or less-than-proportionately. In other words the firm will experience *increasing, constant,* or *diminishing returns* to the variable factor. In a similar manner, long-run changes in output will lead to *economies of scale, constant returns to scale,* or *diseconomies of scale.*

11

Short answer questions

1 To which category of output (see above) does each of the following items belong?

    a A domestic washing machine.   **b** Insurance.

    c A sewing machine in a clothing factory.   **d** Entertainment.

    e Stocks held in a wholesaler's warehouse.   **f** Semi-finished goods.

2 'If land is strictly defined as "the free gifts of nature", then most of the land used by farmers must be described as a combination of land and capital.' Explain.

3 Some of the gifts of nature are replaceable; others are not replaceable. Give some examples of each type.

4 In a fully employed economy what is the opportunity cost of increasing the rate of capital accumulation?

5 The total population of a country is 50 million, 60% of which is in the working-age group. 65% of the working-age group is gainfully employed or seeking work, while 5% of the non-working-age group is employed (people of pensionable age who carry on working). The average number of hours worked per week is 40. What is the weekly supply of labour in this country?

6 What is the most common measure of the productivity of labour?

7 Identify, from the worker's point of view, some of the advantages and disadvantages of the division of labour.

In economics the word *investment* is taken to mean the creation of real capital goods. Questions **8** to **12** are concerned with the following types of, or features of, capital.

(*a*) A farmer's stock of seed potatoes.

(*b*) The total annual output of capital goods.

(*c*) The purchase of existing shares in a company.

(*d*) An automatic telephone exchange.

(*e*) Gross investment *minus* net investment.

(*f*) Capital creation *minus* capital consumption.

Which of the above provide examples of, or definitions of, the following?

  8 Net investment.

  9 Fixed capital.

10 Depreciation.

11 Circulating (or working) capital.

12 Gross investment.

13 Why are **a** a high degree of specialisation and **b** a high degree of factor mobility likely to be conflicting objectives?

14 An entrepreneur wishes to produce 300 tonnes of commodity *X* per week. Each of the following combinations of the factors of production will produce this weekly output.

Method	Units of land	Units of labour	Units of capital
A	5	5	5
B	3	6	7
C	7	7	3
D	3	5	6

a Is there sufficient information here for a profit-maximising entrepreneur to make a decision on which method to use?

b Which method would he definitely *not* use?

15 The question is based on Figure 2 which shows the changes in average and marginal product when varying amounts of labour are combined with fixed quantities of land and capital.

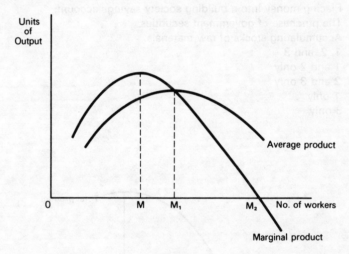

Figure 2

At what employment level is

a total output maximised?

b output per worker maximised?

c the increment in total output resulting from the employment of an additional worker maximised?

16 The inclusion of the entrepreneur as a separate factor of production is sometimes justified on the grounds that the risks borne by the entrepreneur are different in nature from those borne by other types of labour. In what way are they different?

17 Say whether you think the degree of occupational mobility (i.e. the movement from one use or one industry to another) of the following factors is likely to be high or low.

a A blast furnace.

b Unskilled labour.

c A site in the High Street.

d An electric motor.

e A surgeon.

f A single-storey factory building.

18 Distinguish carefully between *diminishing returns* and *diseconomies of scale*.

Multiple choice questions

19 Which of the following would an economist describe as investment?

1 Placing money into a building society savings account.

2 The purchase of government securities.

3 Accumulating stocks of raw materials.

A 1, 2, and 3

B 1 and 2 only

C 2 and 3 only

D 1 only

E 3 only

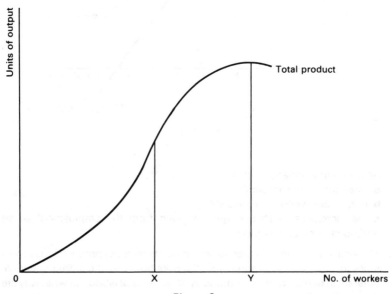

Figure 3

20 The question is based on Figure 3 which shows the changes in total product when different amounts of labour are combined with fixed amounts of land and capital.

Increasing returns to labour are experienced

A over the range of employment 0X.
B over the range of employment 0Y.
C over the range of employment XY.
D only at the employment level 0X.

21 When marginal product is equal to average product,

A average product is rising.
B marginal product is rising.
C average product is at a maximum.
D marginal product is at a maximum.

22 The table below provides information about the inputs and outputs of a firm.

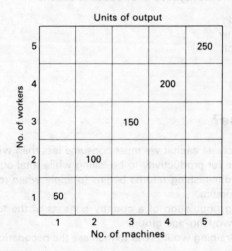

Units of output

The table shows
1 constant returns to labour.
2 constant returns to capital.
3 constant returns to scale.

A 1, 2, and 3
B 1 and 2 only
C 2 and 3 only
D 1 only
E 3 only

23 At the beginning of a particular year a firm had a capital stock of 20 knitting machines. During the course of the year it scrapped 5 and purchased 10 new machines. Which of the following statements is/are correct?
During this particular year, the firm's
1 gross investment in knitting machines was 25 machines.
2 net investment in knitting machines was 5 machines.
3 depreciation amounted to 5 machines.

A 1, 2, and 3
B 1 and 2 only
C 2 and 3 only
D 1 only
E 3 only

24 When a firm using a fixed amount of land and capital takes on more workers it finds that the marginal product of labour falls but the average product of labour rises. This can be explained by the fact(s) that
1 the MP of labour is greater than the AP of labour.
2 the additional workers are more efficient than those already employed.
3 MP and AP always move in opposite directions.

A 1, 2, and 3
B 1 and 2 only
C 2 and 3 only
D 1 only
E 3 only

True or false?

25 a In order to create capital we must consume less than we produce.
b It is possible for productivity to be falling while total output is rising.
c The law of diminishing returns begins to apply when total output has reached a maximum.
d The working population of a country consists of the total number of people in the working-age group.
e Multi-craft training would tend to increase the occupational mobility of labour.
f When a firm is experiencing diminishing returns it means that successive equal increments in output can be achieved with successively smaller increments in inputs.
g The law of diminishing returns is also known as the law of variable proportions.
h Strictly speaking a change in the scale of production means that the proportions between the factors of production remain unchanged.

Data response questions

26 As an economy grows and income per head increases, there is a continuous shift of resources among the different sectors of the economy. For the purposes of this question, economic activities are divided into three very broad groups

(a) agriculture, forestry and fishing, and mining,
(b) manufacture and construction,
(c) services (and all other activities).

Figure 4 gives an approximate indication of the shift of resources as an economy grows. Say which of the above groups of industries are represented by the curves (i), (ii), and (iii), and account for the changes illustrated.

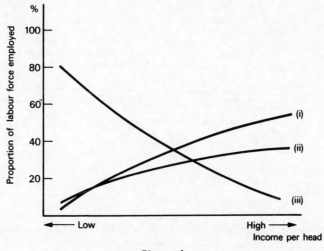

Figure 4

27 The tables below give details of the inputs and outputs of a particular firm over different time periods.

Table A				**Table B**		
No. of men	Units of capital	Units of output (per week)		No. of men	Units of capital	Units of output (per week)
1	1	100		1	1	100
2	1	150		2	2	240
3	1	190		3	3	400
4	1	220		4	4	550
5	1	240		5	5	700
6	1	250		6	6	850

Provide brief explanations of your answers to questions **a**, **b**, and **c** below.

a Which table shows changes in output (i) in the short period, (ii) in the long period?

b Which table illustrates the operation of the law of diminishing returns?

c Which table provides an illustration of economies of scale?

d It is possible to portray the information contained in Table A by means of a conventional graph. Why is it not possible to do the same for the information in Table B?

Part 3
The organisation and scale of production

Introduction

The 'laws' relating to the returns to the variable factor or to the changes in the scale of production refer to changes in *physical* productivity. When the prices of the factors of production are related to these changes in physical productivity, it is possible to get a picture of the way in which costs of production change as output changes. For purposes of analysis, several types of cost must be considered. Total costs are subdivided into *fixed costs* (those not affected by changes in output) and *variable costs* (those which vary directly as output). *Marginal* and *average variable costs* are derived from the marginal and average products. If the prices of the factors of production remain unchanged, then increasing marginal returns will mean that marginal cost will be falling, and vice versa. Similarly movements in average variable cost will be related to movements in the average returns to the variable factor. *Average total cost* will be affected by changes in productivity *and* by the spreading of fixed costs as output changes.

Changes in the scale of production are portrayed by *long-run average cost curves.* Each particular scale of production has its own short-run average cost (AC) curve and the long-run AC curve is derived from the series of short-run AC curves which come into operation as the firm changes from one scale to another. The benefits in the form of lower average costs which arise from the growth in *the size of the firm* are described as *economies of scale* and are usually classified into technical economies, marketing economies, financial economies, adminstrative, and risk-bearing economies. Economies resulting from the growth in *the size of the industry* are described as *external economies.* Increases in the scale of production may eventually lead to *diseconomies of scale* (i.e. AC increases as the scale of production increases).

There are a number of reasons why a firm may attempt to increase its size. Among the more important of these are the desires to achieve (*a*) economies of scale, (*b*) greater market power (the monopoly motive), and (*c*) greater security (by diversification). Growth may be internal but increasingly it takes the form of *integration* (by means of amalgamations and mergers). Over the years the average size of firms has tended to increase, leading, in some industries, to a high degree of *concentration.* In spite of this tendency, however, various limitations on the size of the market have enabled large numbers of small firms to survive and prosper.

From the point of view of the value of output and numbers employed, the *joint stock company* is the most important form of business organisation. There are, however, far more *sole proprietors* than any other form of enterprise. *Partnerships* are important in the professions while *cooperatives* are particularly important in wholesaling and retailing (although *producer* cooperatives are found in manufacturing and farming). State-owned enterprises producing goods and services for the market (i.e. the nationalised industries) are important in mixed economies. These industries are managed by business organisations known as *public corporations*. Important differences between business organisations may be revealed by examining features such as size, ownership and control, sources of finance and motivation.

All firms need to raise funds (*a*) on a short-term basis for working capital, and (*b*) on a long-term basis for fixed capital. There are many sources of finance for firms, the availability of which depends upon such things as the size and credit-worthiness of the firm, the type of business organisation, and the extent of its profitability. A large number of financial institutions of many different types (*the capital market*) exist to provide finance for industry and commerce.

The geographical location of a firm can have an important influence on its costs of production. Certain regions possess *natural advantages* for the conduct of particular economic activities, but once an industry becomes well established in an area, its growth generates important *acquired advantages* for firms (in that industry) operating in that area. In the UK (and most other countries), the government plays an important part in determining the location of industry.

In the UK, *the government's industrial policy* takes the form of (*a*) state ownership and control of industrial enterprises (the nationalised industries), and (*b*) extensive intervention, both positive and negative, in the private sector of the economy. Measures to influence the regional distribution of industry include physical controls and financial inducements. Grants and tax concessions are used as a means of encouraging investment, research and development. Financial assistance has been made available to facilitate the restructuring and modernisation of industry and to help key industries in financial difficulties. Public funds are used to improve and to extend the scope of industrial training.

Short answer questions

1 Which of the following are fixed costs?
   a Depreciation.
   b Insurance of buildings and plant.
   c Wages of operatives.
   d Subsidies on meals provided for the firm's workers.
   e Interest on debentures.
   f Royalties paid by publishers to authors.
2 The question is based on the following table which shows the changes in total cost as output varies in the short run.

Units of output	Total costs (£s)
0	20
1	24
2	30
3	42
4	60
5	80

a Calculate the average variable cost when the output is 3 units.
b Is the firm experiencing increasing or decreasing returns?

3

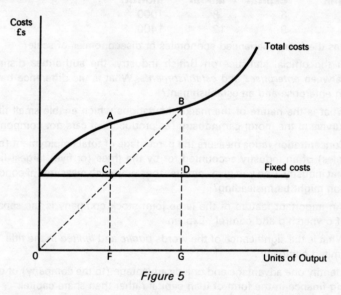

Figure 5

In Figure 5, which particular type of cost is represented by
a AC **b** BG **c** BD/OG **d** CF/OF **e** AF/OF

4 If, as output increases, a firm's total cost_____ at a(an) _____ rate, it means that the firm's marginal cost is falling. What are the missing words?

5 In its production process a firm uses a sequence of four specialised machines A, B, C, and D, each carrying out a different operation. The respective hourly outputs of each machine are as follows.

Machine	A	B	C	D
Output (units per hour)	100	200	240	300

If the firm only needs to produce, say, 100 units per hour, then clearly machines B, C, and D would be under utilised. (In this type of situation a full utilisation of capital can only be achieved by having a fairly large output and using different numbers of each type of machine.)

What is the minimum hourly output required in order to achieve 100 per cent utilisation and what is the minimum number of each machine the firm will need to employ?

6 What economies might be achieved by the merger of a firm making confectionery and a firm making soft drinks?

7 A firm increases its size and output as follows

Units of land	Units of capital	Units of labour	Total output (tonnes per month)
4	6	8	1000
6	9	12	1400

Has the firm experienced economies or diseconomies of scale?

8 In the official statistics on British industry, the authorities distinguish between *enterprises* and *establishments*. What is the difference between an enterprise and an establishment?

9 What is the nature of the market limitations which enable small firms to survive in the motor car industry (as producers of cars not components)?

10 Concentration ratios measure the percentage of total employment (or total sales) of an industry accounted for by the three (or five) largest firms in that industry. Can you give some reasons why such measures of concentration might be misleading?

11 'An important feature of the large joint stock company is the separation of ownership and control.' Explain.

12 What is the significance of the words *public* and *limited* in the title 'public limited company'?

13 Identify one advantage and one disadvantage (to the company) of obtaining finance in the form of loan capital rather than share capital.

14 An important feature of the Stock Exchange is that it provides a degree of _____ for what would otherwise be an _____ asset. What are the missing words?

15 Use the following table to answer the questions below.

Capital Structure of the ABC Co. Ltd
100000	5% Secured Debentures of £1
100000	7½% Preference Shares of £1
200000	Ordinary Shares of £1

a What is the ratio of risk capital to loan capital?
b What is meant by secured debentures?
c If the company has £27500 available for distribution to debenture-holders and shareholders, what ordinary dividend will it declare?

16 Outline briefly the main reasons for government intervention in the location of industry.

17 Give some examples of how the following features of industrial structure, business practices, and market conditions might help the small firm to survive and prosper.
a Disintegration **b** Cooperation **c** Demand for variety

18 'The economic and social obligations of a nationalised industry present the management with conflicting objectives.' Give some examples of situations where this statement might be true.

19 What is the difference between **a** *the dividend*, and **b** *the yield* on a share?

20 One of the main motives for horizontal integration is to carry out a policy of *rationalisation*. What is meant by rationalisation?

Multiple choice questions

21 Which of the following types of amalgamation is/are described as vertical integration?
1   A manufacturer of electric washing machines merges with a firm making refrigerators.
2   A car manufacturer takes over a car body-building plant.
3   A brewery acquires ownership of public houses.

A   1, 2, and 3
B   1 and 2 only
C   2 and 3 only
D   1 only
E   3 only

22 Which of the following is/are examples of external economies of scale?
1   Large firms obtain substantial discounts on their purchases of raw materials.
2   Technical progress leads to development of micro-computers at a price which enables small firms to use them at low cost.
3   A number of independent firms operate as specialist suppliers of services to a particular industry.

A   1, 2, and 3
B   1 and 2 only
C   2 and 3 only
D   1 only
E   3 only

Questions **23**, **24**, **25**, and **26** refer to a very large firm which finds itself able to
A   obtain a high credit rating with financial institutions.
B   produce an output large enough to allow full utilisation of large specialised units of capital.
C   supply a variety of products.
D   achieve a low unit cost on its advertising.
E   maintain a very high load factor with its juggernaut lorries.

Which of the above features is an example of

23 an economy of increased dimensions?

24 an economy arising from indivisibility?

25 a marketing economy?

26 a financial economy?

27 Which of the following is a public corporation?

    A   ICI
    B   NCB
    C   GEC
    D   BP

28 An investor considers a stable income more important than part-ownership and the prospect of capital gains. In which order of preference would he rank the following securities?
1   Ordinary shares
2   Debentures
3   Preference shares

    A   1, 2, 3
    B   2, 1, 3
    C   3, 2, 1
    D   2, 3, 1
    E   1, 3, 2

29 Which of the following groups has the first claim on the assets of a company in the event of it being wound up?

    A   Holders of voting ordinary shares.
    B   Holders of participating preference shares.
    C   Holders of debentures.
    D   Holders of non-voting ordinary shares.

True or false?

30 **a** In the case of the larger companies, retained profits tend to be a minor source of funds for investment.
b Shares in private companies cannot be offered to the general public.
c The existence of some kind of Stock Exchange is essential if the government wishes to sell large quantities of long-term securities.
d Insurance companies and pension funds are the major shareholders in many large UK companies.
e If marginal cost is rising, average cost must also be rising.
f The acquisition of monopoly power is a motive for vertical integration rather than horizontal integration.

g In the case of the cooperative retail societies, ownership is vested in the people who work in these organisations.

h A public company is a company owned by the government.

i A conglomerate is a business organisation controlling subsidiary firms operating in several different industries.

j A large firm's powerful bargaining position in the market for its raw materials is an example of an external economy of scale.

Data response questions

31 The following extracts are taken from a newspaper advertisement by a unit trust (known as 'the X Unit Trust' for this question).

'The X Unit Trust is designed to provide a high and growing income with the prospect of capital appreciation.

'Our investment policy is to concentrate on ordinary shares. In fact, over 90 per cent of the Fund is invested in UK equities. Preference shares with their fixed return and restricted growth potential have been avoided.

'The declared aim of the X Unit Trust is to achieve an income at least 50 per cent higher than the ordinary share average. On Friday the 3rd February the estimated gross yield was 8.46 per cent. This compares with a figure of 5.64 per cent for the *Financial Times* All-Shares Index on the same day.'

a What is a unit trust?

b In the context of this advertisement what is meant by *capital* appreciation?

c Why are preference shares described as having restricted growth potential?

d Under what circumstances might preference shares offer the prospect of capital gains?

e What is meant by gross yield and how is it calculated?

32 A car manufacturer has recently introduced an entirely new model. The research and development costs amounted to £100 million and the cost of new equipment, in the form of machines and the assembly line, was also £100 million. Market research and preliminary advertising accounted for another £40 million. Once production was under way, the variable cost per car was constant at £3000. The car was launched at a manufacturer's selling price of £3500.

a Prepare a graph showing the relationship between average cost and price, as sales and output increase (horizontal scale up to 700000 cars).

b Prepare a graph showing the relationship between total cost and total revenue, as sales and output increase.

c What is the break-even output?

d How do your graphs help to explain car manufacturers' complaints that restrictions on home sales due to higher taxation or hire purchase restrictions seriously handicap their efforts in export markets?

33 The following extracts are taken from the Monopolies and Mergers Commission Report entitled *The Supply of Ready Mixed Concrete*. (Cmnd 8354, 1981.)

(i) 'The nine largest companies in the ready mixed concrete industry all have access to aggregates* either from their own quarries or from those of associated companies. Fifty-eight of the ninety-six small companies which answered our enquiries also obtained some or all of their supply of aggregates from sources which they controlled. Vertical integration is attractive to the ready mixed concrete companies for several reasons.'

(ii) 'Companies which were originally in the aggregate business told us they had moved into concrete because they wished, in the face of vertical integration in the opposite direction, to protect this major outlet for their product.'

(iii) 'It is also possible for vertical integration to inhibit competition.'

a Identify some of the possible reasons why vertical integration is attractive to ready mixed concrete companies.

b Identify the two kinds of vertical integration mentioned in the second quotation and explain, in simple terms, the situation which led the companies to take the action described.

c In what ways might vertical integration in this industry inhibit competition?

---

* Crushed stone or rock.

Part 4

Population

Introduction

The present size and rate of growth of the world's population is a subject of great concern. In many less developed countries the rate of population growth appears to be the major constraint on attempts to raise real income per head.

World population in 1983 was estimated to be in the region of 4.5 billion. It took only thirty-five years for the world's population to rise from 2 billion to 4 billion and the next 2 billion is likely to be added in twenty-five years.

Much of the less developed world is in the earliest stage of *demographic transition*, that is, the stage in which death rates have fallen much further and faster than birth rates so that population growth rates are high (between 2 and 3 per cent per annum). It will probably be many years before these countries reach the stage where death rates have stopped falling while birth rates continue to fall until they are equal to or below death rates, and population becomes stable (as it is in many industrialised countries).

The coexistence of rapid population growth and low standards of living in many parts of the world has revived interest in the population theories of the *Reverend Thomas Malthus* who believed that there is a natural tendency for population to grow faster than the means of subsistence.

A feature of population which is of considerable interest to the economist is the *dependency ratio* which measures the relationship between the numbers in the non-working age groups to the numbers in the working age groups. Since those in the non-working age groups are not income earners, the 'burden' presented by the dependent age groups depends upon the *activity* or *participation rate*, that is, the proportion of the working age group which is gainfully employed.

The proportion of elderly people in the UK has been increasing. A century ago one quarter of the British population was over forty; by 1980, one quarter was over sixty. Future trends in the UK dependency ratio, however, will tend to be more favourable. The number of births per year has been falling since the mid-1960s so that the number of young dependents is tending to fall. The number reaching retirement age will also tend to fall as a result of the falling birth rates during the 1920s.

The idea of an *optimum population* relates the size of population to the supply and quality of the other national economic resources (including technical knowledge).

The size of the working population depends upon the numbers in the total population, the proportion in the working age groups, and the activity rate. Economic and technical changes have brought about important changes in the occupational distribution of the UK working population; the most significant of these has been the shift in employment away from industrial-type activities towards services.

Short answer questions

1 This question is based on the following demographic features.
(i) A low birth rate and a low death rate.
(ii) A low average age.
(iii) A large proportion of young dependants.
Which of the above population features are characteristic of
a a developed industrialised country?
b a low-income African country?

2 Which particular population statistics are calculated using the following formulae?
a The number in the non-working age groups expressed as a percentage of the number in the working age groups.
b The number of deaths, in any one year, of infants aged 0–12 months, per 1000 live births in the same year.

3 Malthus believed that there was a universal tendency for population to grow as a _____ progression.
a What is the missing word?
b According to Malthus, the reason why population failed to grow at this rate was the existence of *positive checks*. What did Malthus mean by positive checks?

4 In the past 25 years in the UK there has been a substantial increase in the number of students in full-time further education. In spite of this trend, the activity rate has not fallen. What major development offset the effects of the growth in full-time further education?

5 Use the following information to make projections of
a the country's population at the end of year 2.
b the country's labour force at the end of year 2.

Population at end of year 1	10 million
Estimated: crude birth rate	20 per thousand
crude death rate	10 per thousand
net immigration	20000 per annum
percentage in working age groups	70 per cent
activity rate	70 per cent

6 'For purposes of economic analysis, population density measured in terms of the number of persons per square mile has little significance.' Explain.

7 An index of ageing is obtained by dividing the population of retirement age and over by the population under 15 (or 16) and multiplying by 100. What would be the implication of an increase in this index for public expenditure on the various social services?

8 In many developing countries 70 per cent or more of the labour force is engaged in agriculture. Productivity, however, is extremely low and the ratio of labour to land is very unfavourable; there is a surplus of labour. In many areas the marginal product of labour is probably negative. The obvious policy is to create more employment off the land. It is difficult, however, to expand non-agricultural outputs rapidly enough to cope with the increase in population *and* to reduce the surplus of agricultural labour.

Suppose, in a particular country, the farm population is 70 per cent of the whole and that population is increasing at 1.5 per cent per annum. At what percentage rate must non-agricultural employment increase if the rural surplus of labour is to be reduced?

Multiple choice questions

9 The term *optimum population* refers to that size of population which, with the country's existing supplies of land, capital, and technical knowledge, will

A maximise total output.
B maximise output per head.
C maximise marginal productivity.
D minimise unemployment.

10 Which of the following will *not* affect the official dependency ratio?

A An increase in the school leaving age.
B A reduction in the official ages of retirement.
C An increase in the activity rate.
D An increase in the birth rate.

11 The working population of the UK expressed as a percentage of the total population is, approximately,

A 75%
B 65%
C 55%
D 45%

12 In the UK, women outnumber men because
1 life expectancy is higher for women than for men.
2 the number of female births exceeds the number of male births.
3 there are more women than men in all age groups.

A 1, 2, and 3
B 1 and 2 only
C 2 and 3 only
D 1 only
E 3 only

13 In the UK, in the past decade, there has been a decline in the numbers employed in
1   manufacturing.
2   agriculture, and mining.
3   the health services.

A   1, 2, and 3
B   1 and 2 only
C   2 and 3 only
D   1 only
E   3 only

True or false?

14 a The number of children in our schools over the next five years can be predicted with a high degree of accuracy.
b Malthus's theory of population was based on the law of diminishing returns.
c A much higher proportion of the population of the UK is economically active than was the case fifty years ago.
d Over the past two decades the growth of world population has outstripped the increase in world food supplies.
e In many less developed countries 40 per cent or more of the population is aged under fifteen years.
f A fall in the birth rate does not necessarily reflect a fall in the fertility rate.

Data response question

15 The question is based on Figure 6 which shows the age composition of the population in two different countries A and B.

From the information provided by Figure 6, what conclusions might be drawn about the differences between Country A and Country B in respect of
a birth rate and death rate?
b life expectancy?
c proportions in working age groups?
d dependency ratio?
e level of economic development?

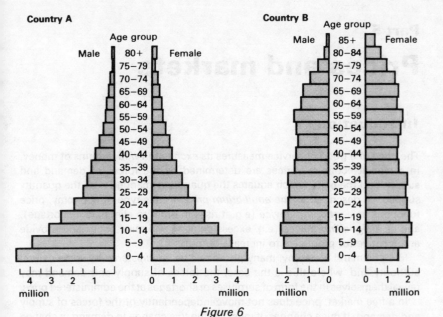

Figure 6

Part 5

Prices and markets

Introduction

The price of a good or service measures its *exchange value* in terms of money. In a market economy, prices are determined by the forces of demand and supply, and the price which equates the quantity demanded with the quantity supplied is described as the *equilibrium price*. In this type of economy, price functions as a *rationing device* (e.g. it rises in order to eliminate a shortage), and as a *signalling device* (e.g. excess demand will raise prices and provide an incentive for producers to increase output).

In a command economy, many prices will be *administered* by some central authority and, where this is the case, the forces of supply and demand may reveal themselves in the form of surpluses or shortages at the administered price.

In a free market, price does not move independently of the forces of supply and demand. If price changes, it must be due to a change in demand, a change in supply, or both. It is important to have a clear understanding of the causes of changes in demand and supply.

In order to describe and explain the extent to which price and quantity are affected by shifts in demand and supply, economists make use of the concepts of *elasticity of supply* and *elasticity of demand*. The measurement of elasticity makes use of *proportionate* changes in quantity and price and *not* absolute changes.

The study of price determination requires a study of different types of market. A *market* is any effective arrangement which enables buyers and sellers to carry out exchange transactions. Markets vary from the small local variety where buyers and sellers meet face to face, to world-wide markets where buyers and sellers conduct their business by making use of a variety of tele-communication systems.

For purposes of economic analysis, markets are differentiated according to the degree of competition within the market. As a yardstick for assessing the extent of competition in real-world markets, economists have devised a model of *perfect competition* which specifies the conditions necessary for the market price to be beyond the influence or control of any one buyer or any one seller. Perfect competition is a theoretical abstraction; it is not found in the real world where markets are described as being imperfect. Real-world markets range from highly competitive ones, which contain some of the features of perfect competition, to *monopoly*, which is the extreme form of imperfect competition. Many markets in the real world are examples of *monopolistic competition* where the use of brand names and competitive advertising gives firms a degree of monopoly power, but this power is severely limited by competition from very similar (but not identical) products. Markets dominated by a few powerful sellers are described as *oligopolies*, while those dominated by a single buyer are known as *monopsonies*.

1 Prices

Short answer questions

1 What are the typical market media (or means) which enable local markets in secondhand houses and secondhand cars to operate effectively?

2 Explain why price is described as a measure of exchange value.

3 'A demand curve presents a picture of intended demand not realised demand.' Explain.

4 'The demand for commodity X is 1000 units.' What further information is required in order to make this a meaningful statement?

5 'Other things being equal, a fall in the price of a commodity will lead to an increase in the quantity demanded.' Name two possible changes in these 'other things' which would make it very difficult to predict the effect of a fall in the price of a commodity.

6 Assuming other things remain equal, which of the changes set out below would
  a cause a movement *along the demand curve* for the commodity?
  b cause a movement *of the demand curve*?
  (i) An increase in the costs of producing the commodity.
  (ii) A fall in a consumers' real income.
  (iii) An increase in the price of a substitute for the commodity.
  (iv) An increase in productivity in the industry producing the commodity.

7 In Figure 7, which of the following changes might be possible causes of the shift of the supply curve from SS to S_1S_1?
  (*a*) The granting of a subsidy to producers.
  (*b*) An increase in the costs of labour and raw materials.
  (*c*) The imposition of a tax on the commodity.

8 Explain the nature of the relationships, illustrated in Figure 8, between
  a good Y and good X (Figure 8(a)).
  b good Y and good Z (Figure 8(b)).

9 In a particular market the short-run supply curve is perfectly inelastic. If demand at all prices increases by 10 per cent, what happens to total revenue?

33

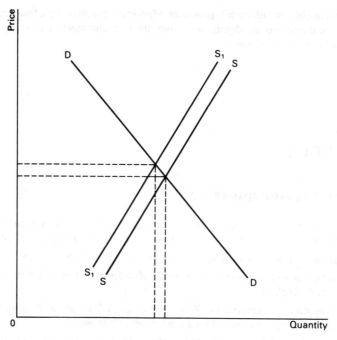

Figure 7

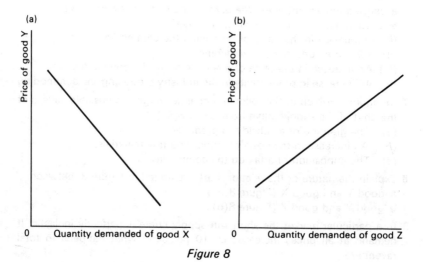

Figure 8

10 Explain why, in the following passage, statement A is wrong and statement B is correct.

'A consumer will maximise the satisfaction which she obtains from her purchases when

A   the same marginal utility is derived from each good purchased.'

B   the same marginal utility is derived from the last pound spent on each good.'

11 The following equation represents the market demand function for good A

$$Q_\alpha = 400 - 5P_\alpha - 0.1\,Y$$

where Q_α is the quantity demanded per week, in thousands of tonnes, P_α is the price of good A, in pounds, and Y is the national income, in billions of pounds.

Is good A

a an inferior good?

b a normal good?

c a Giffen good?

Explain your answer.

12 The question is based on Figure 9 which shows the market demand and supply curves for an agricultural commodity.

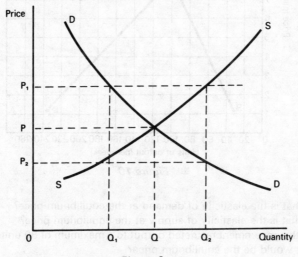

Figure 9

a What is the equilibrium price?

b If the government offered farmers a guaranteed price of $0P_1$, what would be the extent of the market surplus?

c If the government bought the entire output at the guaranteed price and then disposed of it on the open market,

(i) what would be the loss per unit?

(ii) what would be the total loss?

13 The price elasticity of demand for a product is 1.5. To what extent will a fall of 10 per cent in the price of the product affect the quantity demanded?

14 This question refers to the market relationships between commodities A and B. Specify the nature of these relationships in each of the following cases.

a A decrease in the demand for A leads to an increase in the price of B.

b An increase in the costs of producing B leads to an increase in the demand for A.

c A fall in the price of A (due to improved productivity) leads to an increase in the demand for B.

15 This question is based on Figure 10.

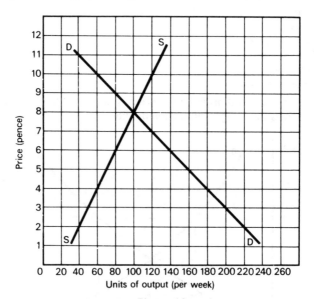

Figure 10

a What is the elasticity of demand at the equilibrium price?

b What is the elasticity of supply at the equilibrium price?

c If the government restricted output to a maximum of 80 units per week, what would be the equilibrium price?

d Returning to the original position, it is assumed that producers have adequate reserve stocks, and while these stocks last they are prepared to meet any increased demand at the current market price. In this situation, what would be

(i) the market price if demand increased by 40 units at all prices?

(ii) the quantity demanded and supplied at the new equilibrium price?

16 Use a supply and demand diagram to show the main reason why the annual sale of Cup Final tickets leads to such widespread dissatisfaction.

17 What conditions give rise to a black market?

18 The imposition of a tax of 4p per unit raises the price of a commodity. In the relevant price range, elasticity of demand is 1.5 and elasticity of supply is 0.5. How much of the tax is borne by the consumer and how much by the producer?

19 The question is based on Figure 11 which shows the effects of granting a subsidy to producers.

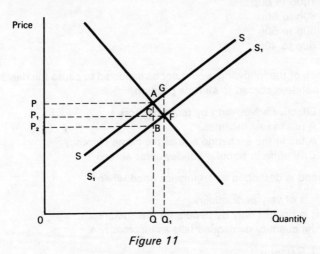

Figure 11

a What is the equilibrium price after the granting of the subsidy?
b To what extent, in terms of price and quantity, have consumers benefited from the subsidy?
c What is the total subsidy payment?
d What is the total revenue received by producers after the payment of the subsidy?

Multiple choice questions

Questions **20** and **21** are based on the following table.

Quantity demanded (per week)	Marginal revenue (pence)
0	
1	100
2	60
3	20
4	20
5	0
6	−20

20 As the price falls from 80p to 60p, demand is

A   inelastic.
B   of unit elasticity.
C   elastic.
D   perfectly elastic.

21 Elasticity of demand is unity in the price range

A   100p to 80p
B   80p to 60p
C   60p to 50p
D   50p to 40p

22 Which of the following would *not* be expected to cause the demand curve for holidays abroad to shift its position?

A   Effective advertising by tour operators.
B   A rise in real incomes.
C   A fall in the exchange rate of the home currency.
D   Civil strife in popular holiday areas abroad.

23 A good is described as an inferior good when

1   it is of very poor quality.
2   it is bought only by people on low incomes.
3   the quantity demanded falls as incomes rise.

A   1, 2, and 3
B   1 and 2 only
C   2 and 3 only
D   1 only
E   3 only

24 The income elasticity of demand for a product is 1.5 at all prices. If real income rises by 6 per cent, the quantity demanded of the product will

A   rise by 9 per cent.
B   fall by 9 per cent.
C   rise by 4 per cent.
D   fall by 4 per cent.

Questions **25** and **26** are based on the following table.

Price (pence)	Quantity demanded (per week)	Quantity supplied (per week)
5	100	60
6	100	80
7	100	100
8	100	120

25 Over the price range given, the demand curve

- A has unit elasticity.
- B is infinitely elastic.
- C has zero elasticity.
- D has an elasticity between 0 and 1.

26 If the government imposes a specific tax of 1p per unit, the new equilibrium price will be

- A 6p
- B 7p
- C 8p
- D somewhere in the range 7p to 8p

Questions **27** to **30** refer to the following changes in the market conditions for a commodity.

A A successful advertising campaign is carried out by producers of a closely competing brand.

B Workers in the industry producing the commodity obtain an increase in wages which is not accompanied by an increase in productivity.

C Horizontal integration in the industry leads to greater economies of scale.

D Unfavourable publicity regarding the health hazards associated with the consumption of a substitute commodity has significant effects on consumers' preferences.

Which of the above is most likely to cause

27 a movement of the demand curve to the left?

28 a movement of the demand curve to the right?

29 a movement of the supply curve to the left?

30 a movement of the supply curve to the right?

31 This question is based on Figure 12 which shows changes in the demand and supply conditions for a commodity.

Initially the market equilibrium was at the point of intersection of the demand curve DD and the supply curve SS. The government then imposed an indirect tax on the commodity and this is the present situation.

Which of the following combinations of changes in equilibrium would result if

(a) the indirect tax were to be replaced by a subsidy, and

(b) consumers also experienced an increase in real income?

- A Y → S → T
- B S → Y → X
- C X → R → S
- D R → X → Y
- E S → Y → Z

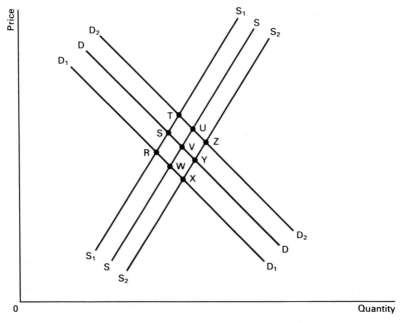

Figure 12

32 A demand curve which takes the form of a straight line sloping downwards from left to right

    A   has unit elasticity at all prices.
    B   has the same elasticity at all prices.
    C   is elastic at higher prices and inelastic at lower prices.
    D   is inelastic at higher prices and elastic at lower prices.

Questions **33** and **34** refer to the equations set out below which represent the demand and supply schedules for commodity X. *P* represents the price of X in pounds, while Q_d and Q_s represent the quantities demanded and supplied per week.

(*a*) $Q_d = 140 - P$
(*b*) $Q_s = 4P - 160$

33 What is the equilibrium price?

    A   £40
    B   £60
    C   £80
    D   £120

34 What quantity will be demanded at the equilibrium price?

    A 20   C 80
    B 60   D 120

True or false?

35 a Any straight-line supply curve which passes through the origin has unit elasticity at all prices.
b Other things being equal, a fall in supply will lead to higher prices unless the demand curve is perfectly elastic.
c The cross elasticity of demand between two substitute goods has a positive value.
d Other things being equal, a fall in price is necessary in order to persuade people to buy more of a good because total utility diminishes as consumption increases.
e When supply is perfectly inelastic, the burden of an indirect tax falls wholly on the purchasers.
f The setting of a maximum price above the equilibrium price will lead to a market surplus.
g The effect of a tax on a commodity is to shift every point on the supply curve vertically upwards by the amount of the tax.
h Farm output and farm revenues will move in opposite directions whenever the demand for the product is inelastic.
i An increase in demand may lead to a higher price in the short-run, but a lower price in the long-run.

Data response questions

36 This question refers to the following quotation.

'If left to themselves, self-contained agricultural product markets show substantial and erratic variations in price because of unplanned changes in output and generally low price elasticity of demand.

'As a result of severe drought conditions in 1975, the volume of potatoes coming on to the British potato market was 20 per cent down on the previous year. A combination of high transport costs and government trade restrictions led to a partial isolation of the home (main-crop) potato market. Potatoes cannot be stored for more than about one year and retail demand is very inelastic. So prices rose by nearly 40 per cent in that year.'

a Using supply and demand diagrams, explain the relationships described in the first paragraph of the quotation.
b What is the relevance of the fact that potatoes cannot be stored for more than one year?
c What was the price elasticity of demand for potatoes in the year to which the quotation refers?
d What happened to the incomes of potato producers in the year in question? Explain your answer.

37 The following quotation is taken from *The Economist*, 13 October 1979.

'Why do commodity prices fluctuate more sharply than prices of manufactures? One reason is the difficulty of varying outputs of primary products. To produce more may require the planting of new fields or the digging of new mines – which takes years rather than months.

'A long period of low prices obviously deters new investment (it is reckoned that copper prices would need to be about 20 per cent higher than now to justify a new mine).

'Producing less is also tricky, at least in the short-run; it would mean destroying some crops which cannot be stored and the costs of storing others are usually high. *It seldom makes sense to reduce mining output, because marginal costs of production (mainly labour) are low compared with capital costs.* And, because market demand is generally insensitive to price changes, the pattern of price instability is reinforced.'

a What does the information in the first and third paragraphs of the quotation tell us about the nature of the short-run supply curves for primary products?
b Explain the relevance of the information in the second paragraph for the engineering industries in the developed countries which might be anticipating a boost in the demand for their products.
c Explain the meaning of the sentence in italics by making use of the relationships between output, variable costs, fixed costs, and total costs.

2 Markets

Short answer questions

38 Why, under conditions of perfect competition, is the demand curve facing *the firm* perfectly elastic while the demand curve facing *the industry* is downward sloping?

39 A firm facing a perfectly elastic demand curve can, in theory, sell an infinite amount at the ruling market price. What, therefore, limits the quantity it sells?

40 The U-shaped cost curves of the individual firm include *normal profit*. What is meant by normal profit?

41 The question is based on Figure 13 which shows the costs and revenue curves of a firm operating under perfect competition.

a At which output will the firm maximise profit per unit?
b Which output maximises total profit?
c Assuming the firm is in equilibrium and is maximising profit, is the situation shown one of short-run or long-run equilibrium? Explain your answer.

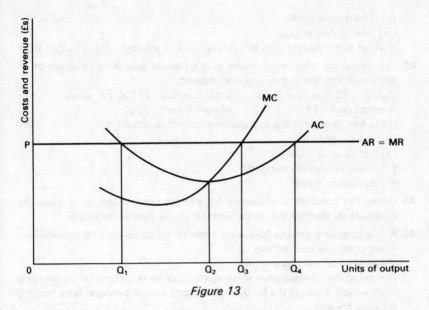

Figure 13

42 The question refers to Figure 14 which shows the total costs and revenue curves of a firm operating under perfect competition.

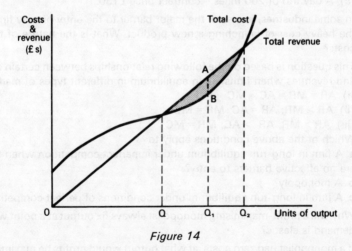

Figure 14

a The total revenue curve begins at the origin, but the total cost curve does not. Why is this?

b What does the gradient of the total revenue curve represent?

c Profit is maximised at the output $0Q_1$. Which of the following represent maximum total profit?

(i) The shaded area.

(ii) The distance AB.

(iii) The distance AQ_1.

d What is the relationship between price and average cost at output OQ_2?

43 The following information refers to the present operating situation of an individual firm trading in a perfect market.

Output 50 units per week   Total revenue   £1000 per week

Average cost   £15   Marginal cost   £20

If the firm is attempting to maximise its profits should it

(*a*) reduce output?

(*b*) increase output?

(*c*) leave output unchanged?

Explain your answer.

44 Using the conditions necessary for perfect competition as a basis for comparison, identify the 'imperfections' in the market for petrol.

45 A bus company has the following costs (the figures are hypothetical).

Fixed costs per bus per day   £15

Variable costs per bus per mile   75p

Assuming the company has some spare capacity (i.e. some buses are lying idle), which, if any, of the following contracts would it accept? Give reasons for your answer.

(*a*) A day trip of 100 miles – contract price £80.

(*b*) A day trip of 70 miles – contract price £70.

(*c*) A day trip of 200 miles – contract price £130.

46 In some industries, it is said, the major barrier to the entry of new firms is the heavy cost of launching a new product. What is the nature of these costs?

47 This question is based on the following relationships between certain costs and revenues when firms are in equilibrium in different types of market.

(i) $AR = MR = AC = MC$

(ii) $AR > MR$; $AR = AC$; $MR = MC$

(iii) $AR > MR$; $AR > AC$; $MR = MC$

Which of the above conditions apply to

a A firm in long-run equilibrium under imperfect competition when there are no effective barriers to entry?

b A monopoly?

c A firm in long-run equilibrium under conditions of perfect competition?

48 Why will a profit-maximising monopolist always fix output at a point where demand is elastic?

49 If a monopolist had zero costs, at what output would profits be maximised? (The output should be identified in terms of the value of MR.)

50 The question is based on Figure 15 which shows costs and revenue curves of a firm operating under imperfect competition.

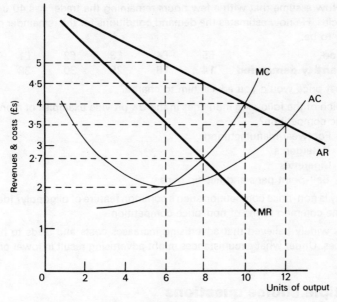

Figure 15

a At which price/output combination would profits be maximised?
b At which of the prices illustrated would the firm be earning no more than normal profits?
c If the firm restricted output to the technical optimum, what profit per unit would it earn?
d If the firm were a public corporation aiming to 'break even', what would be the most likely price/output combination?

51 Figure 15 can be used to show that if a perfectly competitive industry were monopolised, output would be reduced and price would be increased. Can it be assumed that, in practice, this would be the case?

52 a What is meant by discriminating monopoly?
b Explain how discriminating monopolists in the UK use (i) different time periods, and (ii) age differences, as means of creating separate markets.

53 A market trader purchases 100 articles which have been specially made for a particular annual fete. He pays £2 for each of them. If any of the goods remain unsold at the fete they will be virtually unsaleable at any subsequent event. His only other costs are stall fees for the day (£20) and transport costs (£20). He estimates the demand conditions to be as follows:

Price	£5	£4	£3	£2	£1
Quantity demanded	50	80	125	150	200

a Which of the prices indicated would yield the greatest profit?
b Which of the prices would maximise profits if stall fees were increased to £40?

c Now assume that with a few hours remaining the trader has 40 unsold articles. He now estimates the demand conditions for the remainder of the day to be:

Price	£5	£4	£3	£2	£1
Quantity demanded	14	18	25	30	38

What price would you advise him to charge?

54 Which of the following industries in the UK provide examples of monopolistic competition?
  (a) Footwear manufacturing.
  (b) Detergents.
  (c) Cigarettes.
  (d) Ball-point pens and felt-tip pens.

55 Why is non-price competition such a common feature of oligopoly? Identify some common forms of non-price competition.

56 It is widely believed that advertising increases costs and leads to higher prices. Under what circumstances might advertising result in lower prices?

Multiple choice questions

57 Which of the following statements is *incorrect*?
Under perfect competition

A the market demand curve is downward sloping
B the individual firm aims to produce where AC is at a minimum
C a firm may earn abnormal profits in the short-run
D the firm can sell as much as it wishes at the ruling market price

Questions **58**, **59**, and **60** are based on the following market situations.

A Few suppliers – no product differentiation.
B Many suppliers – many real or imagined differences in product.
C Many suppliers – each selling identical products.
D Market dominated by a single buyer.

Which of the above is described as

58 monopsony?

59 perfect oligopoly?

60 perfect competition?

61 The Monopolies and Mergers Commission
  1 can break up existing monopolies and prohibit mergers.
  2 sits as a branch of the High Court.
  3 acts upon references made to it by the Director-General of Fair Trading and the Secretary of State.

A 1, 2, and 3 D 1 only
B 1 and 2 only E 3 only
C 2 and 3 only

Questions **62**, **63**, and **64** refer to the following restrictive trade practices.

A Exclusive dealing and collective boycott.
B Collusive tendering.
C Cartels.
D Pooling of patents.

Which of these practices operate in the following manner?

62 The firms in an industry (or the majority of them) collaborate in the formation of a joint selling agency which is responsible for regulating and marketing the entire output of the member firms.

63 The member firms of a trade association threaten to withdraw all supplies from any market outlet which sells the products of any non-member firm.

64 In contract work the member firms of a trade association share out the work available by restricting price competition.

Questions **65**, **66**, and **67** are based on Figure 16 which shows the costs and revenue curves of a firm operating under imperfect competition.

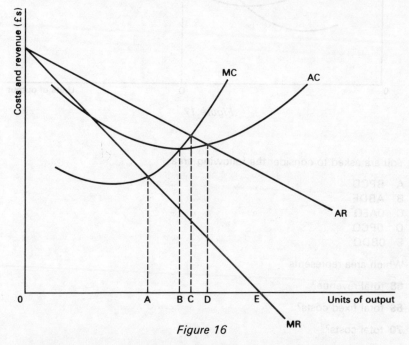

Figure 16

At which of the output levels marked A to E would the firm be

47

65 maximising total revenue?

66 maximising total profit?

67 breaking even?

Questions **68**, **69**, **70** and **71** refer to Figure 17 which shows a firm in short-run equilibrium under conditions of perfect competition.
OP = current market price   ATC = average total cost
AVC = average variable cost   MC = marginal cost

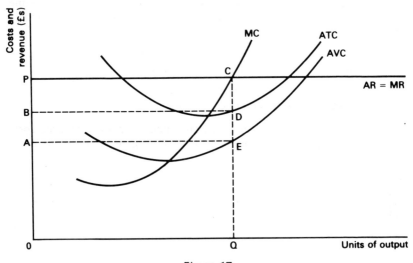

Figure 17

You are asked to consider the following areas.

A   BPCD
B   ABDE
C   0AEQ
D   0PCQ
E   0BDQ

Which area represents

68 total revenue?

69 total fixed costs?

70 total costs?

71 total abnormal profit?

True or false?

72 a A fall in fixed costs would not cause a profit-maximising firm to change its output.

b In the short-run a firm will continue to produce as long as total revenue covers fixed costs.

c A monopoly can only exist where there is a single producer.

d Under perfect competition the market price is fixed.

e Total revenue is at a maximum when marginal revenue is zero.

f All oligopolies are characterised by a severe restriction of price competition.

g In the UK, the legislation on restrictive trade practices applies to the supply of services as well as to the supply of goods.

h A successful advertising campaign will tend to reduce the price elasticity of demand for the product.

Data response questions

73 This question is based on the following extract.

'In mature markets, demand conditions continue to limit policy options. The growing significance of replacement demand in the mature markets for durable products threatens to add to the uncertainty and volatility of corporate performance. The pressure this creates for qualitative innovation and introduction of improved products encourages firms to look for ways to reduce technological risk and, in industries such as aerospace and motor vehicles, demand maturity and rapid technical change interact to produce rationalisation of the product range.

'The motor industry is a major example of a sector where the market is increasingly determined by the level of replacement rather than new demand. With 1.8 persons per car (implying over 2 vehicles per household) in the United States, 3.6 in the United Kingdom and 3.3 in Western Europe as a whole in 1981, the rapidly diminishing marginal utility of an extra vehicle suggests that saturation point has virtually been reached. Moreover, consumers' decisions about when or whether to replace their cars become more crucial to the health of the industry as product durability increases and tastes rather than need can play a greater role in consumption timing.'

(Source: Jump, N. F., 'Competition and Cooperation in Consumer Durable Industries', *Barclays Review* (May 1983).)

a What do you understand by the term *mature markets*?

b Identify some other consumer durables (apart from motor cars) where, in the UK, replacement demand is likely to be a very significant proportion of total demand.

c Explain what is meant by 'rationalisation of the product range'.

d Explain, in more detail, the relationships between 'diminishing marginal utility' and 'saturation point' as they affect the car industry.

e What points made in this quotation help to explain the increased frequency with which motor manufacturers have tended to introduce 'new and improved' models?

74 This question is based on the following table which shows the costs and revenue relating to possible weekly outputs of firm X. The product is a consumer good.

Output (thousands)	Total costs (£000s)	Total revenue (£000s)
4	47	76
5	57	90
6	66	102
7	74	112
8	80	120
9	85	126
10	91	130
11	99	132
12	110	132

a Is this firm operating under perfect or imperfect competition?

b What is the most profitable weekly output?

c Suppose that costs and market demand remain as shown in the table. The firm is now offered a contract to supply a large supermarket with 5000 units per week at a price of £15 per unit. This is an attractive opportunity since it offers the prospect of a long-term contractual relationship.

(i) Should the contract be accepted?

(ii) What, if any, additional output should be sold and at what price?

Give reasons for your answers.

75 An investigation into the activities of a large dominant firm reveals the following facts.

(*a*) It is an efficient large-scale capital-intensive producer.

(*b*) It has a good record in research and development.

(*c*) There is a rapid rate of technical progress in this industry.

(*d*) The firm is protected by a fairly substantial tariff on competing imports.

(*e*) It has a large export business.

(*f*) The prices of the firm's products in the home market are well above average costs and profit margins on home sales are much higher than those for industry in general.

You are asked to write the concluding section of a report on this firm in which you are required to set out recommendations for action by the Secretary of State for Trade and Industry. Give reasons for your recommendations.

Part 6
The national income and its distribution

1 The national income

Introduction

National income is a measure of the flow of real national output over a period of one year. It represents the value of the goods and services becoming available for consumption plus the net additions to the national stock of capital.

National income is always measured at *factor cost*. This differs from market price valuations because many market prices contain elements of indirect taxes and subsidies.

Several important aggregates are derived in the calculation of the national income.

Gross Domestic Product (*GDP*) is a measure of the total output from the factors of production located within the country (some of these factors may be owned by overseas residents).

Gross National Product (*GNP*) is a measure of the total output from factors of production owned by residents of the country. This measure takes account of the income from assets located overseas but owned by residents of the home country and of the income going overseas to foreign owners of assets located in the home country.

National income (or net national product) is equal to GNP *minus* depreciation.

National income accounting is based on the important identity

$$income \equiv output \equiv expenditure$$

This identity represents three different ways of looking at the national income and indicates that there are three different ways of measuring the national product.

(*a*) *The output method* measures national income in terms of the total value of *final* goods and services produced. An alternative approach is to aggregate the *values added* at each stage of production.

(*b*) *The income method* aggregates the incomes paid to factors of production (i.e. wages, interest, rent, and profits) for services rendered in producing the national product.

(*c*) *The expenditure method* takes account of the fact that whatever is produced must be sold or added to stocks. Expenditure on the national output is defined so as to include additions to stocks.

It is most important that the student should clearly understand why these three forms of measurement will yield the same total.

Statisticians are obliged to use money values as their measuring rod in producing estimates of the national income. There is clearly no way of aggregating the physical quantities of the vast range of goods and services produced in an economy. This means that movements in *nominal* national income can be due to (*a*) changes in the volume of output, (*b*) changes in the general level of prices, or (*c*) both volume and price changes.

Since national income data is widely used to indicate changes in standards of living, it is important to have some means of eliminating the effects of price changes in order to obtain some idea of the movements in *real* national income. Index numbers of prices are used for this purpose.

National income statistics are also widely used as a means of comparing standards of living between different countries. The student must be aware of the problems involved in using national income statistics for the purposes mentioned above.

Short answer questions

1 What is the difference between Gross National Product and the national income?

2 Why would it be misleading to calculate national income by adding up the values of the gross outputs of all the enterprises in the economy?

3 Why do we count the incomes derived from UK investments overseas as part of the UK national income?

4 Would the sale price of a secondhand car be counted as part of the national income? Explain your answer.

5 If we are given the sum of all the personal incomes received in one year, what major additions and subtractions would have to be made to this total in order to obtain the national income?

6 Why does the item 'Value of physical increase in stocks and work in progress' appear in the *Expenditure* table in the national income accounts?

7 'In calculating the national income we should not include the salaries of policemen since their incomes are derived from tax revenues and will have been counted elsewhere as part of other people's income. To include the salaries of policemen, therefore, would be a form of double counting.' Explain why this statement is wrong.

8 Which of the following should be included in the national income?
   (*a*) The profits of a dealer in secondhand furniture.
   (*b*) Mr Smith's winnings from gambling.
   (*c*) Interest on debentures.
   (*d*) Students' grants.
   (*e*) A soldier's pay.

(*f*) The estimated rent which an owner-occupied house might yield if it were let to tenants.

9 a Why do the national income statistics omit the productive activities of housewives?

b Does this omission seriously limit the usefulness of the statistics?

10 What proportion of the UK national income represents a return to labour (as distinct from the returns to capital and land)?

11

	Year 1	Year 5
National income (£ million)	10000	20000
Index of prices	100	140

What happened to real national income over this period of time?

12 From the following data calculate:

a the Gross Domestic Product at market prices.

b the Gross National Product at market prices.

c the national income.

	£ million
Consumers' expenditure	50
Public authorities' current expenditure on goods and services	15
Gross domestic fixed capital formation	15
Value of physical increase in stocks	1
Exports	20
Imports	25
Property income paid abroad	1
Property income from abroad	2
Taxes on expenditure	10
Subsidies	3
Depreciation	10

13 Why might changes in real national income provide a misleading indicator of changes in the standard of living?

14 International comparisons of national income statistics usually make use of the current rate of exchange as a means of converting the figures to a common denominator. Why must the information obtained in this way be used with caution?

Multiple choice questions

15 Which of the following is *not* included in estimates of the national income?

A Salaries of civil servants.

B Undistributed profits.

C Investment grants.

D Salesmen's commissions.

An Introductory Economics Workbook

16 Gross National Product at market prices minus Gross Domestic Product at market prices is equal to

A capital consumption.
B net property income from abroad.
C exports *minus* imports.
D stock appreciation.

17 Which of the following is *not* a transfer payment?
A A payment of compensation for fire damage by an insurance company.
B Winnings in the Premium Bonds' lottery.
C Payments to cover capital depreciation.
D Government grants to the universities.

18 A firm closes down and the proprietor, whose total income from the business was £10000 per annum, becomes an employee of another firm at a salary of £6000 per annum. His two assistants, each of whom received a wage of £4000 per annum, lose their jobs; they qualify for unemployment benefit at £2500 per annum. The former proprietor retains ownership of the business premises and lets them at a rental of £2000 per annum. What is the net change in the national income?

A A decrease of £4000 p.a.
B A decrease of £7000 p.a.
C A decrease of £10000 p.a.
D A decrease of £18000 p.a.

19 This question refers to the following information.

	£ million
Capital consumption	1000
Taxes on expenditure	10000
Subsidies	500
National income	50000

GNP at market prices is equal to

A £41500 million.
B £51000 million.
C £59500 million.
D £60500 million.

20 Over a period of five years the following developments took place in an economy.
(*a*) Nominal GNP increased by 20 per cent.
(*b*) The general price level rose by 20 per cent.
(*c*) The population remained unchanged.
Which of the following changes occurred?

54

A   Nominal GNP per head rose, real GNP per head fell.
B   Nominal GNP per head and real GNP per head remained constant.
C   Nominal GNP per head remained constant, real GNP per head fell.
D   Nominal GNP per head rose, real GNP per head remained constant.

Questions **21** and **22** refer to the following items.

A   The total value of the stock of assets owned by residents of the country.
B   The total money supply in the country.
C   The flow of goods and services becoming available to the residents of the country over some given period of time.
D   The aggregate value of all the capital goods in the country.

Which of the above represents

21 the wealth of the economy?

22 the national income?

True or false?

23 a All local authority expenditures financed from local rates are transfer payments.
b An imputed rent is an estimate of the market value of the income from premises occupied by their owners.
c The national income statisticians limit themselves strictly to those items for which there has been a market transaction.
d The sum of the values added at each stage in the production of a commodity will be exactly equal to the sum of the payments made to factors of production for their services in producing that commodity.
e Just as we deduct indirect taxes from the expenditure account, so we must deduct direct taxes from the income account.
f Employers' national insurance contributions are a transfer payment and are not included in the national income.

Data response questions

24 Set out overleaf is a highly simplified system of national income accounts (e.g. there are no subsidies and no property income is paid to or received from abroad). The table shows flows between different sectors of an economy. Each of the separate accounts balances; each item of receipts has a corresponding 'payments' entry in another account and vice versa for payments.
a From this table derive the Gross National Product at factor cost as (i) an income account, and (ii) an expenditure account.
b Comment on this form of presenting the national income accounts.

Receipts	£ million	Payments	£ million
THE HOUSEHOLDS' ACCOUNT			
Sale of factor services to firms	20000	Consumption spending	16000
		Saving	2000
		Taxes on income	2000
	20000		20000
THE FIRMS' ACCOUNT			
Sale of consumption goods and services to households	16000	Purchases of factor services from households	20000
Sales to government	4000	Imports	4500
Gross investment	4000	Retained profits	1000
Exports	4000	Indirect taxes	1000
		Profits tax	1500
	28000		28000
THE GOVERNMENT'S ACCOUNT			
Taxes on households' income	2000	Purchases from firms	4000
Profits tax	1500	Budget surplus	500
Indirect taxes	1000		
	4500		4500
CAPITAL ACCOUNT			
Savings by households	2000	Capital formation (gross investment)	4000
Savings by firms	1000		
Budget surplus	500		
Overseas borrowing	500		
	4000		4000
THE REST OF THE WORLD ACCOUNT			
Exports	4500	Imports	4000
		Loans	500
	4500		4500

25 Figure 18 gives a very simplified picture of the flows of goods, services, and money payments between the firms in an industry and between those firms and households. The figures refer to thousands of pounds.

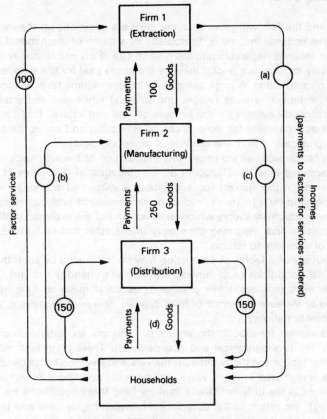

Figure 18

a What are the missing numbers at (a), (b), (c), and (d)?
b What is the total contribution to national income?
c Explain how Figure 18 may be used to demonstrate the fact that the sum of the values added = value of final products.

2 Wages

Introduction

In this and the following two sections there are questions on the manner in which the national income is distributed. How much of the national income a person receives depends upon the relative size of his or her money income. But money incomes are prices; they are the prices paid for the services of the factors of production. A large part of total money income takes the form of a reward for labour services (wages and salaries) while rent and interest are paid to property owners for the services of land and capital. Profit may also be seen as a payment for the services of risk-taking and enterprise but also as a surplus gained from the exercise of monopoly power.

Since factor incomes are prices, any explanation of the way such incomes are determined must take account of the operation of the forces of supply and demand in the markets for land, labour, capital, and enterprise. A study of the demand for a factor of production requires some understanding of the marginal productivity theory which takes account of the expected profitability of production and, assuming the supply of the other factors is fixed, of the effects of diminishing returns.

The supply of a factor of production may be influenced by such things as geological conditions (e.g. minerals), population changes (labour), institutional barriers (e.g. restrictive practices), technical restraints (e.g. the time required to increase the stock of fixed capital), and educational and training requirements (labour).

In the market for labour, the problems of supply are largely problems of mobility (both geographical and occupational). There is, in fact, no single market for labour but many different markets and the mobility between these markets is restricted in many ways. Although the conditions of demand will be different in the different labour markets (and these conditions are always changing), the extent of the differentials between highly-paid and low-paid occupations would clearly be substantially reduced if labour could move easily from one occupation to another.

The demand for labour is a function of its productivity and the value of its product. Technical progress plays an important part in determining the demand for labour in many markets. A firm's demand for labour is significantly affected by its ability to substitute capital for labour, depending, of course, on the relative costs.

An important feature of the process of wage determination in the UK is the existence of trade unions and the procedure of collective bargaining. Trade unions exercise considerable power in the markets for labour by virtue of their ability to influence the supply of particular types of labour.

Short answer questions

26 What would happen to the MRP curve of a factor of production if
  a its physical productivity increased?
  b the price of its product fell?

27 Figure 19 shows the ARP and MRP curves for labour employed by an individual firm. OW is the market wage rate.

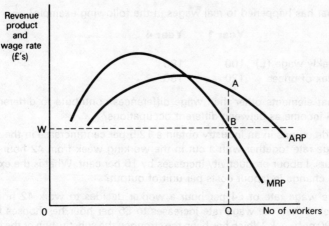

Figure 19

  a What is the total reward to labour?
  b What is the total value of labour's product?
  c Which part of Figure 19 represents the firm's demand curve for labour?
  d What does the horizontal wage line tell us about the supply of labour to this firm?

28 The following table shows the variations in output as a profit-maximising firm with fixed amounts of land and capital employs more labour. The product sells at a price of £5 per unit.

No. of workers	Total output (units per week)
1	20
2	46
3	76
4	103
5	122
6	132

How many men would be employed
a at a wage of £100 per week?
b at a wage of £145 per week?

29 Which of the following features would tend to make the *demand* for labour
  a elastic?
  b inelastic?
  (i) Wages form a small proportion of total costs.
  (ii) The product is in competition with a number of close substitutes.
  (iii) Labour is highly skilled and requires a long training period.
  (iv) Low-cost labour-saving machinery becomes available to the industry.

30 If labour were perfectly mobile both occupationally and geographically,
  would the wage rate be the same for all occupations?

31 What has happened to real wages in the following example?

	Year 1	Year 4
Weekly wage (£)	100	180
Index of prices	120	150

32 What elements other than wage differences contribute to differences in
  real income as between different occupations?

33 Trade unions in an industry obtain a 12.5 per cent increase in the weekly
  wage rate together with a cut in the working week from 42 hours to 40
  hours. Labour productivity increases by 10 per cent. What is the extent of
  the change in labour costs per unit of output?

34 At a wage rate of £4 per hour a worker decides to work 42 hours per
  week. When the wage rate increases to £5 per hour he chooses to earn
  £190 per week. Which has been the stronger, the substitution or the income
  effect?

35 'The curve showing the amounts of labour supplied by any individual at
  different wage rates may well be backward-bending, but this will not be
  true of the supply of labour to an industry.' Why not?

36 Which of the following trade union policies aim **a** to shift the supply curve
  for labour to the left, **b** move the demand curve for labour to the right?
  (i) Insisting on a long apprenticeship period.
  (ii) Putting restrictions on the use of labour-saving equipment (e.g.
  overmanning).
  (iii) Using political pressure to obtain more effective protection against
  imports.

37 In which of the following occupations would you expect the supply of
  labour to be inelastic? Give reasons for answers.
  (*a*) Surgeon.
  (*b*) Railway porter.
  (*c*) Underwriters at Lloyds in the City of London.
  (*d*) Architect.
  (*e*) Van driver.

Multiple choice questions

38 In order to increase his labour force from 10 men to 11 men, an entrepreneur is obliged to raise the weekly wage rate from £100 to £104. The marginal cost of labour is

A £4.00
B £44.00
C £104.00
D £144.00

39 'Smith gets a much higher wage than Jones because he has had a much longer period of training.'
On the question of the determination of wage differentials, this statement provides
A a satisfactory explanation; a long period of training entitles a person to a higher wage.
B a satisfactory explanation because Smith will be much more skilled than Jones.
C an unsatisfactory explanation because it only deals with factors which affect supply.
D an unsatisfactory explanation because it only deals with factors which affect demand.

Questions **40** and **41** relate to Figure 20 in which DD and SS represent the market demand and supply curves for building workers. Initially the market is in equilibrium when the wage rate is 0W, and 0M workers are employed.

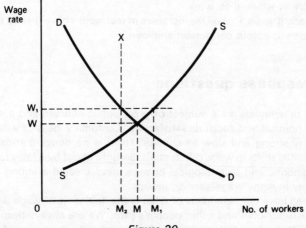

Figure 20

40 Which of the following is likely to lead to the employment of $0M_1$ workers at a wage rate of $0W_1$?

A   Trade unions enforcing a minimum wage of $0W_1$.
B   An increase in the availability of building land and a fall in its price.
C   The government establishing a minimum wage of $0W_1$.
D   A fall in the numbers of workers seeking jobs in this industry.

41 If, in the initial market situation, the trade unions restricted the supply of workers to $0M_2$, which of the following would be correct statements?
1   XM_2 would be the new supply curve of labour.
2   The wage rate would rise to $0W_1$.
3    $0M_2$ workers would receive a rise in wages.

A   1, 2, and 3
B   1 and 2 only
C   2 and 3 only
D   1 only
E   3 only

True or false?

42 a More than half the UK working population are members of trade unions affiliated to the TUC.
b The indexation of wage rates is a device which attempts to prevent a fall in real wages during periods of inflation.
c A wages policy which only allows equal flat-rate increases for all workers gradually erodes wage differentials.
d The UK and the countries of Western Europe have very similar trade union structures because they all organise workers on the basis of the industry in which they work.
e In recent years, in the UK, increases in real wages have greatly exceeded increases in output per person employed.

Data response questions

43 Wage differentials are a subject of great public concern and a source of much political and social dissatisfaction. Customary ideas of what is 'fair' are very strong and slow to change. There is no doubt that recent and substantial shifts in wage differentials, brought about by a fairly rapid pace of economic and technological change, have created a strong sense of inequity in many wage-earning groups.

We all have our own ideas of what is the 'fair' or 'just' wage differential between our own and other people's jobs. We are always hearing complaints that jobs which are 'hard' often command a lower rate of pay than some jobs which seem to be 'easy', or that jobs which require a longer period of training are paid less than some jobs which require little or no training.

There seems to be much public support for some kind of *job evaluation* whereby the different aspects of an occupation can be evaluated in such a way that some sensible comparison between jobs can be made and then used as a basis for establishing wage differentials. Set out below is a very simple hypothetical example of the techniques of job evaluation. The different requirements of jobs are specified and a maximum number of points is awarded to each feature (10 points, say, where the feature is very prominent, 5 for moderate intensity, and 0 where the feature is not present at all). The maximum number of points is not the same for all features – they are weighted. 'Experience' might rate a maximum of 20, while 'monotony' has a maximum of 5 points.

		Assessment of job	
Feature	Maximum points	A	B
Previous experience	20	15	—
Learning period	15	10	2
Reasoning ability	20	15	4
Dexterity	12	4	4
Responsibility for materials and equipment	10	4	2
Teamwork	8	2	5
Attention to detail (orders, blueprints etc.)	10	6	1
Monotony	5	—	4
Abnormal effort	10	1	5
Disagreeableness	15	2	10
Risk (i) injury	15	1	3
(ii) disease	10	1	2
		61	42

What views is an economist likely to have on the use of this technique as a basis for establishing a framework of wage differentials?

44 The following excerpts are taken from 'Will Pay Follow Prices?', *Lloyds Bank Economic Bulletin, No. 47*, November 1982.

'The 1981–82 pay round ending in July resulted in an average rise of 10.8 per cent in earnings per person employed in all industries. The increase in wage rates in the 1981–82 pay round was only 7.6 per cent.'
'Those employed in manufacturing did 2 per cent better than the average, increasing their earnings by 12.9 per cent in the pay round even though their weekly wage rates rose by only 7 per cent.'

'There was a remarkable increase in manufacturing productivity during the pay round. Output per person employed went up by 8.3 per cent. Output per person/hour rose less, by 5.9 per cent. Wages and salaries per unit of output thus rose by only 4.2 per cent, compared with the 12.9 increase per person.'

'During the 1981–82 pay round (8/81–7/82), the general price level rose by 10.7 per cent.'

a Explain the discrepancy between the movements in earnings and movements in wage rates described in the first two paragraphs of the quotation.

b Why did output per person employed rise by more than output per person per hour?

c Use the numerical data in the quotation to explain the relationships between earnings and labour costs.

d What happened to (i) real earnings, (ii) real wage rates, in manufacturing industry during the period covered by the information in the quotation?

3 Interest

Introduction

We now turn to those incomes which accrue to a group of people widely known as capitalists. They are the owners of property who hire out their capital and land for use in the production of goods and services and who bear the financial risks involved in these activities. Incomes derived from the ownership of property take the form of interest, rent, and profits.

The rate of interest may be defined as the price of capital, or more realistically as the rate which must be paid in order to acquire the funds needed to purchase capital equipment. If the firm is using its own money to purchase capital goods, the current rate of interest is a measure of the opportunity cost of committing these funds to investment. The rate of interest is perhaps best regarded as the price of a loan because in addition to the demand for new capital, loans are demanded for the purchase of existing assets (e.g. second-hand houses) and for durable consumer goods.

One theory of the rate of interest sees it as a price determined by the supply of and demand for loanable funds where the supply of such funds depends upon the level of savings and the creation of additional supplies of money by the banking system.

Another theory of the rate of interest is the monetary or liquidity preference theory which says that the rate of interest is determined by the demand for money *to hold* (i.e. liquidity preference) and the supply of money. It deals with the advantages of holding money as an asset and sees the rate of interest as the price which must be paid to persuade people to forego these advantages.

Short answer questions

45 'The rate of interest may be regarded as the payment which is necessary to overcome people's time preference.' Explain this statement.

46 Figure 21 shows the marginal productivity of capital in relation to the volume of investment. This curve represents the demand curve for capital.

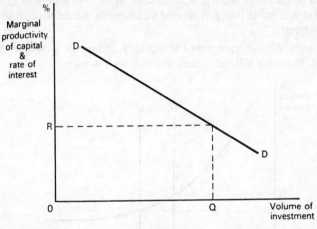

Figure 21

a Explain how the marginal productivity of capital comes to be measured in percentage terms.

b Why does the demand curve slope downwards?

c Why is this demand curve 'grounded in uncertainty'?

d Why would an increase in the rate of interest tend to reduce the amount of capital demanded?

47 What would happen to the demand curve in Figure 21 if

a technical progress made possible a great improvement in the efficiency of capital?

b there was a fall in the demand for the products of this industry?

c entrepreneurs' expectations were seriously influenced by the publication of a pessimistic long-term economic forecast?

48 What are the main determinants of the level of personal savings?

49 State briefly why there is not likely to be a close positive relationship between the level of total saving and the rate of interest.

50 What is the opportunity cost of holding money balances?

51 Distinguish between *active* and *idle* balances.

52 a On what grounds might speculators attempt to increase their money balances?

b What actions would they take in order to achieve their objective?

c How would these actions affect the rate of interest?

53 A person holds 1000 fixed-interest (5 per cent) long-term bonds which were purchased at their nominal value of £100 each. If the market rate of interest now increases to 6.25 per cent, what happens to the market value of these bonds?

54 The price of 2.5 per cent Consols (nominal value £100) stands at £40. What is the market rate of interest?

55 If the government undertook large sales of its own securities in the open market and other things remained equal, what would happen to the rate of interest?

56 In Figure 22, LL represents the liquidity preference schedule. MM and M_1M_1 represent different levels of the money supply.

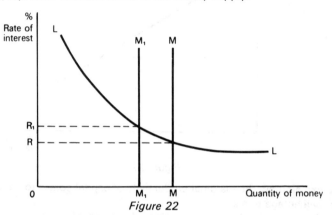

Figure 22

a Why does the liquidity preference schedule flatten (i.e. become horizontal) at a positive rate of interest?

b Why is there a low demand for money to hold when the rate of interest is relatively high?

c When the supply of money is reduced from MM to M_1M_1, the rate of interest rises from OR to OR_1. Explain briefly the real-world events which bring about this change in the rate of interest.

57 What would happen to the demand for money (liquidity preference) if a large number of employees opted to be paid monthly instead of weekly?

58 At the current level of national income, a community wishes to hold £1000 million for transactions purposes and £800 million for precautionary purposes. The speculative demand for money is as follows.

Rate of interest (%)	Speculative demand (£ million)
6	6000
7	5000
8	4200
9	3700
10	3400

What supply of money will give rise to a rate of interest of 8 per cent?

Multiple choice questions

59 If the government finds that it has to make an interest payment of £3.60 on a loan of £100 for 3 months, the short-term rate of interest is

A 1.2 per cent
B 3.6 per cent
C 10.8 per cent
D 14.4 per cent

60 A worker's pay increases from £112 to £140 per week and, at the same time, he agrees to be paid monthly (every four weeks) instead of weekly. If he spends all his income evenly over the pay period, his average holding of money

A remains unchanged.
B increases from £16 to £20.
C increases from £56 to £280.
D increases from £112 to £560.

61 Which of the following is *not* likely to cause a shift of the liquidity preference curve?

A A change in national income.
B Influential forecasts of substantial price reductions.
C A loss of confidence in money as a store of value.
D The central bank undertakes large purchases of securities in the open market.

62 Other things being equal, which of the following is most likely to cause a rise in the market rate of interest?

A An increase in the proportion of income saved.
B An increase in the money supply.
C A substantial increase in the government's borrowing from the non-bank sector.
D A fall in the speculative demand for money.

63 The statement that the demand for money is perfectly interest-inelastic means that

A the propensity to consume is not influenced by changes in the rate of interest.
B the demand for money is the same at all levels of income.
C the rate of interest is fixed.
D changes in the rate of interest will not influence people's liquidity preference.

True or false?

64 a Active money balances are those held for speculative purposes.

b The market rate of interest varies inversely as the price of fixed-interest securities.

c The rates of interest charged to different borrowers vary according to the creditworthiness of the borrower and the duration of the loan.

d The rate of interest which the government pays when it borrows by issuing Treasury bills is known as the bank rate.

e The marginal productivity (or efficiency) of capital is an estimate of the expected future profitability of any additions to the capital stock.

f It is possible for the real rate of interest to be negative.

g Firms can avoid the interest costs of investment if they use their own funds.

h If, at the current price level, there are more willing sellers of bonds than willing buyers, interest rates will rise.

Data response questions

65 Building societies are very reluctant to change mortgage rates. One reason is the administrative cost and inconvenience involved, but probably more important reasons are that the housing market is politically very sensitive, and building societies feel some moral obligation to existing borrowers.

However, if the building societies are unwilling to carry out frequent adjustments to their lending rates, they will be unable to make frequent adjustments to the rates they pay to their depositors. But the inflow of funds into the building societies is very sensitive to the interest rates offered and how they compare with interest rates offered on rival assets such as bank deposit accounts and government securities.

These other rates are much more flexible, so that the rates offered to depositors by building societies become uncompetitive when interest rates in general are rising. Conversely the rates offered by building societies are very tempting when the general trend of interest rates is downwards.

Discuss the likely effects of this state of affairs on **a** house prices, and **b** house building.

66 When considering new outlays on capital goods, entrepreneurs are faced with many uncertainties. They are trying to look into the future and although they can make use of statistical data on past and current trends and the techniques of market research, the economic changes which might take place during the life of the investment are matters for conjecture. For this reason firms often work on the basis of some 'pay-off' or 'pay-back' period. The shorter the period over which the investment is made to pay for itself, the smaller is the risk element.

An investment of £100000 is being considered and capital charges consist of two elements: (*a*) the rate of interest; (*b*) depreciation.

Depreciation is spread evenly over the pay-back period (e.g. if pay-back period is 5 years, then £20000 will be set aside each year to cover depreciation allowances).

a Assuming the rate of interest is 10 per cent, work out the annual capital charges on this investment project if the pay-back period is (i) 5 years (ii) 20 years.

b Carry out the same calculations but assume the rate of interest is 12 per cent. What conclusions may be drawn from this example on the way that investment projects are influenced by changes in the rate of interest?

4 Rent and profit

Rent

Short answer questions

67 'Rent may be defined as a surplus over and above a factor's supply price, or alternatively as a surplus over a factor's opportunity cost.' Explain briefly why both definitions are acceptable statements.

68 In his theory of rent, Ricardo was anxious to demonstrate that rent is 'price-determined' and not 'price-determining'. State briefly what he meant by this assertion.

69 This question is based on the following table

Weekly wage	Number of workers offering services
£100	1
£105	2
£110	3
£115	4

When four workers are employed at a weekly wage of £115, what is the amount of economic rent in total wages?

70 Is it possible for economic rent to be negative? Explain your answer.

71 'Since land is limited in supply, the whole of its earnings takes the form of economic rent.' Is this true? Explain your answer.

72 Why is abnormal profit regarded as a form of economic rent?

73 In its current use (agriculture) a plot of land has a market value of £2000. A nearby town is growing and the plot is now scheduled as building land. Its market value rises to £10000.

a What is the amount of economic rent in the new valuation?

b Suppose that, before the development takes place, the government introduces a development tax of 50 per cent on increments in land values.

(i) Will the tax reduce the supply of this land for development?

(ii) Will the tax raise the price of this land?

74 This question is based on Figure 23 which shows the situation in the market for three different factors of production. In the case of Figure 23(c), assume the factor has only one use.

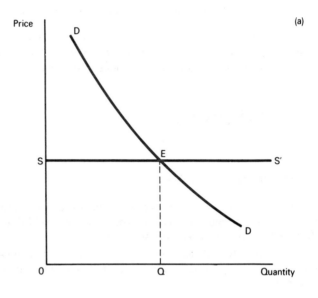

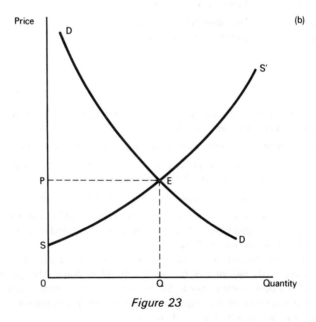

Figure 23

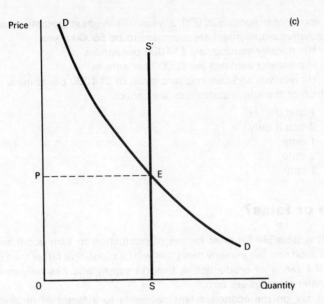

Which areas represent economic rent in the total rewards to the factors of production
a in Figure 23(a)?
b in Figure 23(b)?
c in Figure 23(c)?

Multiple choice questions

75 Which of the following is *not* true?
Economic rent may be defined as the difference between the market price of a factor of production and its

A supply price.
B transfer earnings.
C cost of production.
D opportunity cost.

76 It is estimated that a vacant building in the High Street would be capable of providing its owner with a rental of
1 £20000 per annum if it were used as a supermarket.
2 £15000 per annum if it were used as a night club.
3 £10000 per annum if it were used as a cinema.
If the owner were to allow it to be used as a supermarket, the economic rent would be

A £20000 per annum. C £10000 per annum.
B £15000 per annum. D £5000 per annum.

77 A sports star earns £20000 a year. His highest potential earnings in alternative employment are estimated to be £6000 a year.
1   His transfer earnings are £14000 per annum.
2   His transfer earnings are £6000 per annum.
3   He receives an economic rent equal to £14000 per annum.
Which of the above statements are correct

A   1 and 3 only
B   2 and 3 only
C   1 only
D   2 only
E   3 only

True or false?

78 a It is possible for most factors of production to earn economic rent in the short run, but in many cases this will be quasi-rent rather than pure rent.
b If a factor of production is fixed in supply and has only one use, its transfer earnings are zero.
c A tax on the economic rent payments to a factor of production will reduce the supply of that factor.
d Since profits are surpluses, all profits are a form of economic rent.

Profit

Short answer questions

79 a 'Profits and losses play a crucial signalling role in a free market system.' Explain.
b Identify at least two other functions of profits in a capitalist system.

80 Mr Jones is capable of earning a wage of £8500 a year as a skilled plumber. He decided to use his savings of £7500 (earning interest at 8 per cent per annum) to purchase a plumbing firm. In the first year his revenue was £22000 and his paid-out costs (materials, heating, lighting, transport, etc.) amounted to £9000. He declared that he had made a profit of £13000. Would an economist agree with him? Explain your answer.

81 Firm A   **Firm B**

Profit = 10% on selling price   Profit = 20% on selling price
Capital   Capital
  employed   £20000   employed   £50000
Annual sales £100000   Annual sales   £100000

a Calculate (i) each firm's total profit, (ii) each firm's total profit as a return on capital employed.
b Which of these firms is most likely to be in (i) the quality fashion trade, (ii) the grocery trade?

82 A monopolist's abnormal profits are, on average, £20000 per annum. The government decide to levy a lump sum tax of £10000 per annum on these profits. What effects would this tax have on the monopolist's price and output?

83 What are the main disadvantages, in a capitalist system, of a tax on profits?

Multiple choice questions

84 Which of the following statements is *not* true?
Profit differs from other forms of income in that

A   it may be negative.
B   it is not a contractual payment.
C   the economist does not include any profit in costs.
D   it is subject to much wider fluctuations.

85 A company declares a dividend of 15 per cent. The financial press announces that this is equivalent to a yield of 10 per cent on the current market price of the shares (nominal value £1). The current market price of the shares is

A   £1.10
B   £1.15
C   £1.25
D   £1.50

86 Normal profit is

A   the average rate of profit for the industry.
B   equal to total revenue – total cost (where this difference is a positive item).
C   the supply price of entrepreneurship.
D   equal to average cost.

True or false?

87 a The existence of long-run abnormal profit implies some degree of monopoly power.

b A tax on profit raises the firm's average cost curve.

c Economic theories on the working of the capitalist system assume that all firms try to maximise profit per unit of output.

d Pure profit represents any excess of revenues over all opportunity cost.

Data response questions

88 The following extract is from an article on a West German publishing firm which appeared in *The Economist*, 26 March 1977.

> 'The profit-sharing scheme is open to all employees with more than three years service. Mr Mohn firmly believes that labour should primarily be rewarded by wages and social benefits. But the entrepreneur should not collect all the profits. A return of 20 per cent on the capital employed is deducted for the shareholders – and the balance is reckoned as the group's surplus profit. At Bertelsmann, half of this goes to the employees, half to the shareholders. This year each member of the fund reaped 102 per cent of his June 1976 pay.'

Can this system be reconciled with the traditional views of the nature of and functions of profits under capitalism?

89 The following passage consists of excerpts from an article entitled 'Mixed blessings from the North Sea', *Economist Brief: Britain's Economy Under Strain*, 1982.

> 'However, there are two equally strong arguments for taxing oil companies on their profits.
>
> 'One concerns the economic rent obtained from the North Sea; if companies were prepared to explore and produce before the 1979–80 price rise, they should still be happy with the same profitability. The higher price rise represents a windfall whose cause lay in Iran's revolution; North Sea oil companies should not be the only ones to benefit from it.
>
> 'Linked to that, the government has a delicate balancing act to perform.
>
> 'When oil prices rose sharply ... oil consumers lost, oil producers gained. To restore the balance, the government needs to tax away some or all of the producers' gains, returning it to the consumers in the form of lower taxes or higher benefits.'

a Explain how the Iranian revolution led to windfall gains for oil producers and why these gains are described as economic rent.

b What would be the likely effects on output and prices of the proposed taxation of the profits arising from the sharp increase in oil prices?

Part 7
Money and banking

1 Money

Introduction

The main function of money is to serve as a medium of exchange. This means that money may be defined as anything which is generally acceptable in exchange for goods and services. Money, however, has other important functions. It acts as a store of wealth, serves as a unit of account or measure of value, and is used as a standard for deferred payments.

Over the years all kinds of commodities have served as money, but in most countries today the money supply consists of coins, banknotes, and bank deposits. Nevertheless, there is no general agreement on what exactly constitutes the money supply. If we stick rigidly to the definition of money as a medium of exchange then clearly it includes coins, notes, and bank deposits held on current account (i.e. sight deposits) because these are items which are immediately 'spendable' (although cheques are not universally acceptable).

Most definitions of money also include time deposits held with banks. There are, however, many assets which fulfil some, but not all, of the functions of money. These assets (e.g. building society deposits are sometimes referred to as 'near money' because they possess a high degree of liquidity. They can easily and quickly be turned into a medium of exchange (coins, notes, and bank deposits).

There is no group of assets which economists would unanimously agree upon as constituting the stock of money. For this reason we find that the monetary authorities use several different aggregates to measure the stock of money.

Short answer questions

1 If money is defined as a medium of exchange, which of the following would count as money?
  (a) Anything which is legal tender.
  (b) A bank deposit which is transferable by cheque.
  (c) A postal order.
  (d) A deposit in the National Girobank.

2 The commodity chosen to serve as money must possess certain characteristics if it is to function efficiently as money. What are these characteristics?

3 'Modern banking began when goldsmiths realised that they were sitting on vast quantities of idle wealth while at the same time people were paying usurious rates of interest to moneylenders.' To what developments does this quotation refer?

4 'In the early days of banking there were many spectacular financial crashes in which banks were pushed into insolvency, not because they were *bankrupt* but because they were *illiquid*.'
Explain the distinction, in this particular context, between the words in italics.

5 'The fact that there is now no physical gold-backing to the money supply does not mean that there is no backing.' What is the nature of the backing of the money supply in the UK?

6 It has been said that it is misleading to describe the banks as 'creators' of money because all they do is to exchange a liquid asset for an illiquid asset. Is this a correct statement? Explain your answer.

7 What are **a** the major advantages, and **b** the major disadvantages of holding money as an asset?

8 'Every loan creates a deposit.' Explain why this is true of bank lending.

9 The early 'quantity theory' held that changes in the price level were directly proportional to changes in the money supply. What assumptions does this theory make about T and V?

10 If banks always maintain a supply of liquid assets at some minimum level which is equal to a given percentage of total deposits, and
r represents this liquid assets ratio in percentage terms,
D represents the maximum possible level of bank deposits, and
LA represents the amount of liquid assets held by the banks,
write down a formula expressing the value of D in terms of LA and r.

11 What is the relationship between the supply of money and total expenditure during some given period of time?

Multiple choice questions

12 In choosing a commodity to serve as money, which of the following is the most important characteristic? It *must* be

A   issued by the state.
B   easily recognisable.
C   generally acceptable.
D   divisible.

13 Which of the following serve as a medium of exchange?
1 Banknotes.
2 Sight deposits.
3 Cheques.

A 1, 2, and 3
B 1 and 2 only
C 2 and 3 only
D 1 only
E 3 only

14 If a state decreed that one 'new' franc was worth 100 'old' francs, which of the following statements are correct?
1 The value of people's savings would fall.
2 Relative prices would remain unchanged.
3 Prices (in francs) would fall.

A 1, 2, and 3
B 1 and 2 only
C 2 and 3 only
D 1 only
E 3 only

15 A banking system is obliged to maintain 10 per cent of its deposits in the form of cash and always lends out the remainder in the form of advances. If a new deposit of £10 million cash is made into the banking system and the public's demand for cash remains unchanged, what will be the value of the additional deposits created by bank lending?

A £9 million
B £10 million
C £90 million
D £100 million

16 This question is based on the following data.

Year	V	T	P	M
1	100	100	100	100
4	100	110		140

According to the 'quantity theory of money' identity what would be the approximate value of the index of prices in year 4?
A 79
B 127
C 130
D 154

True or false?

17 a Gresham's law states that good money drives out bad money.

b Legal tender is anything which must be accepted in legal settlement of a money debt.

c A nation's money supply is part of the national wealth.

d In the official definitions of the money supply, M1 includes coins, notes, and all bank deposits (both demand and time deposits) held by the public and the private sectors.

e Other things being equal, an increase in the demand for money will lead to a fall in V.

f When a bank makes a loan, its assets and liabilities increase by equal amounts.

Data response question

18 'Much discussion of money involves a heavy overlay of priestly incantation. Some of this is deliberate. Those who talk of money and teach about it and make their living by it gain prestige, esteem and pecuniary return, as does a doctor or a witch doctor, from cultivating the belief that they are in a privileged association with the occult – they have insights that are nowise available to the ordinary person. Though professionally rewarding and personally profitable, this too is a well-established form of fraud. There is nothing about money that cannot be understood by the person of reasonable curiosity, diligence and intelligence.

'It will be asked in this connection if a book on the history of money should not begin with some definition of what money really is. What makes this strip of intrinsically worthless paper useful in exchange, yet leaves another piece of similar size without any such worth? The precedents for such efforts are not encouraging. Television interviewers with a reputation for penetrating thought regularly begin interviews with economists with the question: "Now tell me, just what is money anyway?" The answers are invariably incoherent. Teachers of elementary economics or money and banking begin with definitions of genuine subtlety. These are then carefully transcribed, painfully memorised and mercifully forgotten.'

(J. K. Galbraith, *Money*, Pelican)

Comment on the views expressed here and say whether you agree with them. How would you answer the question posed by the TV interviewer?

2 The banking mechanism

Introduction

The main functions of the banks may be briefly summarised as follows:

(a) to act as a safe deposit,
(b) to issue banknotes,
(c) to provide a means of transmitting money (the cheque system),
(d) to make loans.

In addition, the banking system provides a wide range of other services such as the provision of foreign exchange, the management of invested funds, investment advice, and so on. The power to issue notes is usually confined to the central bank, which also has the responsibility of supervising the work of the whole banking system.

There are several types of bank (central banks, commercial banks, merchant banks, savings banks) and a wide range of other financial institutions which carry out some banking functions. In this chapter we are mainly concerned with the central bank, the commercial (or deposit) banks and the discount houses, because these institutions are the ones principally involved with the creation and control of the money supply. In this connection we must see the Bank of England as an agent of the government, acting ultimately under instructions from the Treasury.

Short answer questions

19 List five major functions of the Bank of England.

20 The note issue appears as a liability on the weekly return from the Issue Department of the Bank of England. What is the nature of this liability?

21 Explain the meaning of the following terms:
  a discounting.
  b base rate.
  c 'accepting' a bill of exchange.

22 Distinguish between the *cash ratio* and *operational* deposits held by the commercial banks at the Bank of England.

23 Why are profitability and liquidity conflicting objectives for the banker?

24 What is the first action taken by the commercial banks when their cash reserves fall below the desired level?

25 Are the restrictions imposed by the Bank of England the only restraints on the banks' ability to increase the level of bank deposits?

26 If the deposit banks' *investments* can be sold at any time on the Stock Exchange, why are they not counted as liquid assets?

27 'The first question to be asked about the structure of British banking is why there should have been such a strong concentration into a small number of very large banks each with many branches. The answer lies simply enough in the economies of scale which exist in banking.' What are these economies of scale?

28 In borrowing from a bank why would a businessman normally prefer overdraft facilities to a bank loan?

29 'Banks have supplies of very liquid assets which enable them to make good, quickly and easily, any depletion of their cash reserves.' If this is so, why is it that a 'loss' of cash might well force the banks to reduce their level of deposits?

30 The Bank of England is a 'lender of last resort'. Which institutions take advantage of this facility?

31 What is the main function of the *inter-bank market*?

32 Why has the Bank of England insisted that all eligible banks above a certain size maintain some minimum level of loans with the members of the London Discount Market Association?

33 What is a *Euro-dollar*?

34 Which items are included in the £M3 definition of the money supply but not in M1?

Multiple choice questions

35 Which of the following items would the banks count as liquid assets?
1   Treasury bills.
2   Notes and coin in the banks' tills.
3   Operational deposits held in the Bank of England.

A   1, 2, and 3
B   1 and 2 only
C   2 and 3 only
D   1 only
E   3 only

36 Which of the following bank assets earn(s) no income?
1   Special deposits held at the Bank of England.
2   Cash ratio deposits held at the Bank of England.
3   Notes and coin.

A   1, 2, and 3
B   1 and 2 only
C   2 and 3 only
D   1 only
E   3 only

Questions **37**, **38** and **39** relate to the following items which have been extracted from a bank's balance sheet.

A Special deposits.
B Money at call.
C Customers' deposits.
D Advances.
E Treasury bills discounted.

37 Which item is a liability?

38 Which is the most profitable asset?

39 Which is the most liquid asset?

Questions **40** and **41** refer to the following transactions carried out by members of the public holding accounts with the clearing banks. All payments are made by cheque.
1 They buy a new issue of government securities.
2 They sell securities to the central bank.
3 They buy existing securities on the Stock Exchange from institutions which also have accounts with the clearing banks.

40 Which of the above transactions would tend to lead to a contraction of bank deposits?

A 1 only
B 2 only
C 3 only
D 1 and 3 only
E 2 and 3 only

41 Which transactions would tend to leave the level of bank deposits unchanged?

A 1 only
B 2 only
C 3 only
D 1 and 2 only
E 2 and 3 only

Questions **42** and **43** are based on the following table which gives details of various components of the UK money supply in 1983.

	£ million
Notes and coin in circulation	11 531
Private sector sterling sight deposits	30 616
Private sector sterling time deposits	55 817
Public sector sterling deposits	2 485
UK residents' deposits in other currencies	14 688

42 The money supply as defined by M1 amounted to
A   £11 531 million   C   £97 964 million
B   £42 147 million   D   £100 449 million

43 The money supply as defined by £M3 amounted to
A   £42 147 million   C   £100 449 million
B   £97 964 million   D   £115 137 million

44 When a discount house purchases a bill of exchange which has three months to run to maturity, *the rate of discount* is equal to

A $\dfrac{\text{nominal value} - \text{purchase price}}{\text{nominal value}} \times \dfrac{100}{1}$

B $\dfrac{\text{purchase price}}{\text{nominal value}} \times \dfrac{100}{1}$

C $\dfrac{\text{nominal value} - \text{purchase price}}{\text{purchase price}} \times \dfrac{100}{1} \times \dfrac{4}{1}$

D $\dfrac{\text{nominal value} - \text{purchase price}}{\text{nominal value}} \times \dfrac{100}{1} \times \dfrac{4}{1}$

Data response question

45 The following table is an example of a weekly return from the banking department of the Bank of England.

Banking department

Liabilities	£ million	Assets	£ million
Public deposits	37	Government securities	1150
Special deposits	711	Advances and other	
Bankers' deposits		accounts	871
operational	199	Premises, equipment, and	
cash ratio	500	other securities	1060
Reserves and other		Notes and coin	7
accounts	1626		
Capital	15		
	——		——
	3088		3088
	——		——

a Explain briefly what each item represents.
b Assuming that other things remain unchanged, explain the initial effects of the following transactions on the items of this balance sheet.
(i) A commercial bank withdraws £1 million in new notes.
(ii) The central bank releases £100 million of special deposits.
(iii) The central bank sells £50 million of securities on the open market to the non-bank public.

3 Monetary policy

Introduction

In attempts to achieve their economic policy objectives, governments make use of a number of different policy tools, including fiscal policy, monetary policy and, sometimes, direct controls over prices and/or incomes. Monetary policy is based on the belief that such things as the amount of money in circulation, or the level of interest rates, can have important effects on the development of the economy.

The main purpose of monetary policy is to regulate the level of aggregate money demand because the level of demand has an important influence on such things as output, employment, and inflation. While the responsibility for the use of monetary policy and the extent to which it is used lies with the government, the task of operating monetary policy is delegated to the Bank of England.

Monetary policy has received increasing attention in recent years. This has been due to the growing influence of the views of monetarists and the fact that the Conservative government elected in the UK in 1979 chose to make the control of the money supply a major feature of its economic policy.

Short answer questions

46 'The net flow, day by day, of government payments and receipts is the main cause of ease or stringency in the money market.'
Explain this statement by means of two simple examples showing the effects on the banking system of **a** a government receipt, and **b** a government payment.

47 What is meant by the statement 'the market was forced into the Bank'?

48 Distinguish between the *targets* of monetary policy and the *instruments* of monetary policy.

49 'The authorities can adjust their basic instruments of control in order to achieve a certain level and structure of interest rates *or* a certain rate of growth of the money supply. But they cannot do both.' What is the reasoning behind this statement?

50 'There have been periods of tight monetary policy when the rate of interest was 5 per cent and times of easy monetary policy when the rate of interest was 10 per cent.' What possible economic conditions might explain the situations described here?

51 One of the great problems in using monetary policy (and indeed other economic policies) is the operation of 'lags' between the time when a change of policy becomes necessary and the time when the policy becomes effective. Can you identify the nature of these time lags?

52 'If the banking system believes that the central bank will enforce penal borrowing whenever interest rates fall more than the authorities wish, money market institutions will take steps to ensure that interest rates do not fall below the desired level.'

a What is meant by penal borrowing?

b How can the central bank enforce penal borrowing?

c What institutions are *directly* affected by the threat of enforced penal borrowing?

d Why should the prospect of penal borrowing prevent the market rate of interest falling below the level desired by the monetary authorities?

53 Government economic policy has several aims as far as the level of interest rates is concerned. The following are three important aims

(i) influencing the external balance,

(ii) minimising the costs of servicing the national debt,

(iii) controlling aggregate demand.

Illustrate with fairly simple examples how

a objective (i) might conflict with objective (ii)

b objective (i) might conflict with objective (iii).

54 In 1981 the Bank of England ceased the practice of setting a publicly announced minimum lending rate. It announced that its future policy would be to keep very short-term interest rates within a narrow unpublished band. What methods does the Bank of England use to achieve this objective?

55 In 1981 the obligation on the banks to maintain a minimum reserve assets ratio was abolished. What new reserve requirement was imposed on the banks?

56 Monetarists argue against the use of discretionary monetary policy as an instrument for 'fine-tuning' the economy. What is the basis of their objections?

Multiple choice questions

57 When the central bank carries out a *funding* operation it means that

A the central bank issues more long-term securities and fewer Treasury bills.

B the central bank issues more Treasury bills and fewer long-term securities.

C the government is running a large deficit and financing it by borrowing from the banks.

D the authorities are providing funds for the commercial banks by purchasing securities from them.

58 If there is a heavy flow of tax payments to the Exchequer, and other things remain equal,

    A the government will need to issue more Treasury bills to offset this flow of money.

    B the banks' cash reserves will be falling.

    C since the payments are made by cheque, the total deposits of the commercial banks will be unaffected.

    D bankers' deposits at the Bank of England will be increasing.

59 Which of the following is/are features of a restrictionist monetary policy?

    1 An increase in income tax.

    2 A call for special deposits.

    3 Open market purchases of securities by the central bank.

    4 A rise in interest rates.

    A 1 and 2

    B 2 and 3

    C 1 and 3

    D 2 and 4

    E 1 and 4

60 Direct controls on the banks in the form of 'lending ceilings'

    1 tend to inhibit competition between the banks.

    2 will have a fairly predictable effect on bank lending.

    3 make use of the price mechanism as a means of restricting bank lending.

    A 1, 2, and 3

    B 1 and 2 only

    C 2 and 3 only

    D 1 only

    E 3 only

61 When the UK operates with a floating exchange rate, an increase in the rate of interest is likely to

    1 lead to a fall in investment by domestic firms.

    2 increase the demand for pounds in the foreign exchange market.

    3 make exports more competitive in overseas markets.

    A 1, 2, and 3

    B 1 and 2 only

    C 2 and 3 only

    D 1 only

    E 3 only

True or false?

62 a The Bank of England influences the supply of money by exercising a strict control on the supply of new banknotes and coins.

b An increase in the supply of money will increase the demand for bonds and hence raise the rate of interest.

c If the banks increase their lending and at the same time sell securities to the public, there will be no overall increase in the stock of money.

d When the stock of money is chosen as a target for monetary policy, a major problem is to decide which financial assets should be included in the target aggregate.

e Open market sales of securities by the central bank will tend to lower the rate of interest.

f The cash ratio deposits held at the Bank of England represent the working balances of the clearing banks.

g With a given monetary target, the level of interest rates will be higher, the higher the PSBR.

Data response questions

63 'But what is the money system? Broadly there are three levels in the economy concerned in the system:

(*a*) at the base the productive activity of firms and consumption by individuals, both requiring credit and money;

(*b*) above these the banks and other financial institutions which provide credit and money; and

(*c*) above the banks the government in the form of the Bank of England supporting the system.

'The word of a banker can initiate economic activity, for production begins with credit. The instruments of monetary policy are a means of restricting advances or the ability of bankers to make promises to pay. In other words they are controls on the money supply, since the deposits which are 90 per cent of the money supply are created directly by advances.

'But the concept of a supply of money can be misleading. *Promises to pay are not produced on a production line, they arise from the judgement of bankers*. Government monetary policy emphasises the quantitative control of the money supply, when what may be needed is qualitative control of bankers' promises. Bankers may give advances to finance production, speculation, the buying of land, or the purchase of paper assets like property bonds. The banking crises of 1974 showed the consequences of granting advances to pay for "investment" which merely drives up land and property values. The point was made recently in an article in a bank review, "many monetarists focus exclusively on the overall growth in money supply and disregard its sources ... this obscures some important policy consequences which must result from different patterns of monetary expansion".

'A banker who finances production can be repaid out of production, whereas a banker who finances a rise in asset values may never be repaid.'

(Adapted from an article in *British Economy Survey*, Vol. 5 No. 1, OUP)

a Explain exactly what is meant by the first sentence of the second paragraph 'The word of a banker ...'.
b Explain the sentence in italics and show the relevance of this statement to the assets side of the banker's balance sheet.
c Give some examples of the type of speculation which may be financed by a bank loan.
d Express your views on the idea that government monetary policy should act on the quality as well as the quantity of bank advances.

64 This question is based on the following quotations taken from *The Bank of England Quarterly Bulletin*, December 1983.

1 'The main expansionary influence on the broad monetary aggregates was the high PSBR; monetary policy operations were therefore aimed at maintaining a sufficient rate of government funding to offset this influence.'
2 'In the event, further heavy gilt-edged sales were achieved without preventing a further fall in yields.'
3 'On that basis, and in the light of other indicators of monetary conditions, the authorities acquiesced on the 3rd October in a ½% fall in short-term interest rates.'

a What is meant by *government funding* and how might this reduce the expansionary influences on the money supply?
b Explain the events described in quotation 2 in terms of the demand for securities, the supply of securities, and the yields on securities.
c What exactly is meant by 'the authorities acquiesced ... in a ... fall in short-term interest rates'?

Part 8

Changes in the value of money – inflation

Introduction

In economics we are concerned with *exchange values*. The value of a commodity is measured in terms of the goods and services for which it can be exchanged. Most goods and services have money prices and these prices are measures of the exchange values of the different goods and services. The same principle applies to the value of money; the value of £1 can only be expressed in terms of those things for which £1 will exchange.

The value of money, therefore, varies inversely as the prices of goods and services and if all prices moved in the same direction and to the same extent, there would be no difficulty in measuring changes in the value of money. If all prices were to double, the exchange rates between different goods would be unchanged; one pound of coffee would be worth exactly the same number of pounds of sugar. The only value which would be changed would be the value of money itself. The exchange value of £1 would be halved.

Unfortunately prices move at different rates and sometimes in different directions. This gives rise to some difficult problems when we attempt to measure what is happening to the value of money. But people want to know what is happening to the real values of wages, pensions, the national income, and other important economic variables. We also need to know something about the causes of changes in the value of money because such changes have important economic and social effects. In recent years the rate at which the value of money is changing has become one of the most important economic statistics.

Short answer questions

1 If the general price level increases by 25 per cent, to what extent would the value of money change?

2 What information is used as the basis for calculating the weights in the Retail Prices Index?

3 Assume that the average shopping basket of goods and services costs £75 per week and that expenditure on meat accounts for £7.50. If the price of meat now rises by 10 per cent, what happens to the index of retail prices? (Assume other prices remain unchanged.)

4 Use the following data to determine the price index for year 2. Assume that the index stood at 100 in year 1 and that the weights are based on expenditure in year 1.

Commodity	Quantity purchased (units)	Prices Year 1	Year 2
A	200	£1.00	£1.20
B	500	10p	15p
C	50	£5.00	£4.00

5 Under what circumstances might an increase in the supply of money have no effect on the value of money?

6 Ordinary shares and property are widely regarded as *a good hedge* against inflation. What is meant by the term in italics?

7 Demand-pull inflation occurs when aggregate demand is allowed to exceed aggregate supply at the current level of prices. Assuming a fully employed economy and, in each case, that other things remain equal, identify three possible causes of excess demand.

8 Economists speak of a *trade-off* between unemployment and demand inflation. What do they mean by this term?

9 Cost-push inflation is often explained in terms of persistent and successful wage claims which force up costs and prices. It can be shown, however, that if other things remain equal and wages increase by no more than the amounts necessary to compensate for the increase in prices, the inflationary sequence will peter out. Demonstrate the truth of this statement by means of a simple arithmetical example.

10 Identify two possible *initiating* causes of cost-push inflation other than excessive wage settlements.

11 In trying to deal with demand inflation by measures which reduce aggregate demand, governments have encountered difficulties because prices have displayed little or no flexibility in a downward direction.
a Why is it that prices do not display the same flexibility when demand is decreased as they do when demand is increased?
b If prices do not fall when demand is decreased, what consequences must follow?

12 a What relationship is portrayed by the Phillips curve?
b It is now believed that either (i) the relationships demonstrated by the Phillips curve no longer hold true in the long run, or (ii) the curve has moved a long way to the right. If (ii) is assumed to be correct, what developments might explain the shift of the curve?

13 What are the main features of the economic condition commonly described as *stagflation*?

14 Economists who do not accept the view that an increase in the money supply is a major *cause* of inflation do recognise the fact that inflation can only continue if the price increases are *validated* (*or accommodated*) *by the government's monetary policy.*
To what action does the expression in italics refer?

15 Theories of demand inflation make use of the concept of *excess demand.* How might the degree of excess demand be estimated or measured?

16 Monetarists assert that, only in the short-period, can an increase in aggregate demand reduce unemployment below *the natural rate.* Their arguments are based on discrepancies which arise between the expected rate of inflation and the actual rate. Explain, briefly, how such a discrepancy can lead to a temporary fall in unemployment.

Multiple choice questions

17 In the Retail Prices Index

    A   the prices of all consumer goods and services are included.
    B   the commodities are weighted according to the quantities of each purchased by consumers.
    C   the prices used in the calculations are retail prices minus indirect taxes.
    D   the weights are revised each year.

Questions **18, 19, 20** and **21** refer to the following terms.

    A   Hyperinflation
    B   Reflation
    C   Deflation
    D   Suppressed inflation

In each of the questions **18–21**, state which of these terms refers to the situations described.

18 A situation where excess demand shows itself by queues, waiting lists and long order books, and other rationing devices.

19 A policy aimed at reducing the level of economic activity.

20 A situation where prices are rising at a phenomenal rate.

21 A policy aimed at increasing the level of economic activity.

22 Which of the following is the most likely cause of cost-push inflation?

    A   A budget deficit.
    B   An expansion of bank credit.
    C   Devaluation.
    D   A large export surplus.

23 This question is based on the following table

Commodity	Consumer expenditure Year 1 (£ million)	Price index Year 1	Price index Year 2
A	200	100	150
B	300	100	80
C	500	100	120

The calculation of a *weighted* price index shows that between year 1 and year 2, the general level of prices has risen by

A 50 per cent.
B 16.66 per cent.
C 14 per cent.
D 5 per cent.

24 Which of the following statements about inflation are true?
1 It eases the burden of the existing National Debt to the government.
2 It can only be sustained in the longer period if the money supply is allowed to increase.
3 It is an inevitable consequence of increasing wage rates.

A 1, 2, and 3
B 1 and 2 only
C 2 and 3 only
D 1 only
E 3 only

25 Which of the following is most likely to be a contributory cause of demand inflation?

A Devaluation.
B A balance of payments deficit.
C A budget deficit.
D An increase in liquidity preference.

True or false?

26 a The idea that an increase in the money supply leads to inflationary pressures is based on the view that money is demanded mainly for transaction purposes.
b During periods of inflation, creditors tend to be 'gainers' and debtors tend to be 'losers'.
c There is general agreement among economists that expectations are an important element in the inflationary process.

d Inflation, by raising the cost of living, inevitably leads to a fall in the standard of living.

e Inflation is a tax on savings.

f Inflation only occurs when an economy has reached a situation of full employment.

Data response question

27 Figure 24 attempts to bring together the main initiating causes of inflation and to show how these causes lead to and maintain the inflationary process.

a Does the diagram illustrate both demand-pull and cost-push processes? Explain your answer.

b The diagram indicates that whatever the initiating cause of inflation, the process itself has one central ingredient. What is this ingredient? (*Clue:* there is no direct link between excess demand and prices.)

Explain how and why this factor is common to both types of inflation.

c Write a short account of the role of expectations in the inflationary process, basing your explanation on the linkages shown in the diagram.

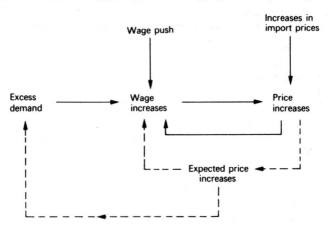

Figure 24

(Source: A. R. Prest and D. J. Coppock (eds), *The UK Economy: A Manual of Applied Economics*, 6th edn, Weidenfeld and Nicolson)

Part 9

International trade, finance and cooperation

1 International trade

Introduction

International trade arises because of the gains to be derived from specialised production. Since there are different factor endowments in the different regions of the world we must expect a diversity in the conditions of production between different countries. Each country might, given the benefits of modern technology, be able to produce some quantity of every commodity, but clearly in many cases it could only be done at enormous cost. Common sense tells us that countries will tend to specialise in those economic activities in which they have some kind of advantage.

International trade develops because

(a) there is an uneven geographical distribution of economic resources;
(b) these resources are relatively immobile between nations;
(c) different commodities require different combinations of resources.

Most of the present patterns of international trade have developed because differences in productive efficiency between countries have revealed themselves in cost differences and hence in price differences. To a great extent the market mechanism has operated to determine the present structure of international specialisation and trade, although this does not apply to much of the trade between command economies and even in the non-communist world there are many restrictions on international trade.

Although there is a great deal of international specialisation we must note that trade between countries is not based solely on the principle of *absolute* advantage. Countries do import goods which they could produce for themselves and some of these goods they could produce more efficiently than the countries from whom they are importing. It is the principle of *comparative* advantage which lies at the basis of international trade.

Short answer questions

Questions **1**, **2**, and **3** are based on a simplified model of a world economy in which there are only two countries (A and B) each producing only two commodities, food and clothing. We assume that resources in each country are mobile between industries, that there are no barriers to trade, and that there are no transport costs. Each question is a separate exercise and uses different data.

1 With an input of x resources, the production possibilities in each country are

	Food (units)		Clothing (units)
Country A	100	*or*	10
Country B	64	*or*	8

a Which country has a comparative advantage in the production of clothing?

b In country A the opportunity cost of producing a unit of food is _____ than in country B. What is the missing word?

2

	Units of resources required to produce	
	One unit of food	One unit of clothing
Country A	2	4
Country B	4	6

a Which country has an absolute advantage in both industries?

b Which country has a comparative advantage in the production of clothing?

c Which of the following terms of trade would be advantageous for both countries?

	Units of food		Units of clothing
(i)	1	for	1
(ii)	7	for	4
(iii)	2	for	1
(iv)	3	for	2

3 Using exactly the same inputs of resources, country A could produce either 12 units of food or 8 units of clothing, while country B could produce either 9 units of food or 6 units of clothing.

Is it possible for both countries to gain from specialising and trading with each other? Explain your answer.

4 'Britain can produce wheat more efficiently in her factories than she can on most of her farmland.'

Taken literally this statement is nonsense, but it does attempt to express important economic realities. Formulate these realities in more precise economic terms.

Questions **5**, **6**, **7**, and **8** are based on Figure 25 which shows the different combinations of goods available to a country (*a*) before it specialises and trades, and (*b*) after it specialises and trades.

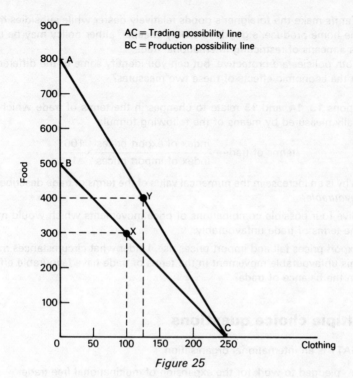

Figure 25

5 What is the *domestic* opportunity cost of one unit of clothing?

6 What are the international terms of trade?

7 In order to move from X to Y, the country
(*a*) specialises in clothing production and exchanges clothing for food.
(*b*) specialises in food production and exchanges food for clothing.
Which is the correct statement?

8 When it has settled at Y, what quantities of which good does the country
a export, and **b** import?

9 Two of the best-known arguments for restricting international trade are
(*a*) the infant industry argument, and (*b*) the strategic argument. Explain
briefly the bases of these arguments.

10 Tariffs may be imposed in the form of *ad valorem* duties or *specific* duties.
Why would specific tariffs tend to discriminate against manufactured
imports from low-wage, low-cost developing countries?

11 Why might governments regard the high degree of specialisation which is
encouraged by free international trade to be an undesirable development?

12 'Tariffs make the foreigner's goods relatively dearer while subsidies make the home producer's goods relatively cheaper; either policy may be used as a means of restricting international trade.'
Both policies are protective, but can you identify some of the differences in the economic effects of these two measures?

Questions **13**, **14**, and **15** relate to changes in the terms of trade which are normally measured by means of the following formula

$$\text{terms of trade} = \frac{\text{index of export prices}}{\text{index of import prices}} \times \frac{100}{1}$$

13 Why is an increase in the numerical value of the terms of trade described as *favourable*?

14 Give four possible combinations of price movements which would move the terms of trade unfavourably.

15 Export prices fall and import prices rise. Under what circumstances might this unfavourable movement in the terms of trade have favourable effects on the balance of trade?

Multiple choice questions

16 GATT is an international organisation

A pledged to work for the expansion of multinational free trade.
B committed to work for the establishment of fixed exchange rates.
C in the form of a customs union linking the USSR and the communist countries of Eastern Europe.
D designed to provide long-term loans on favourable terms to developing countries.

17 A truly prohibitive tariff designed to protect a domestic industry will
1 bring in a substantial revenue for the government.
2 raise the prices paid by the domestic consumer.
3 raise incomes and employment in the protected industry.

A 1, 2, and 3
B 1 and 2
C 2 and 3
D 1 only
E 3 only

18 Which of the following statements is/are *incorrect*?
1 A tariff will raise the prices of imported goods in the home market whereas a quota has no effect on prices in the home market.
2 Quotas, but not tariffs, can be used selectively.
3 A higher rate of tariff will raise more revenue if the demand for the imported good is inelastic.

A   1, 2, and 3
B   1 and 2 only
C   2 and 3 only
D   1 only
E   3 only

19 An adverse movement in the terms of trade means that

A   the volume of exports has fallen relative to the volume of imports.
B   the total value of exports has fallen relative to the total value of imports.
C   the average price of exports has fallen relative to the average price of imports.
D   the balance of trade has moved from a surplus to a deficit.

20 Figure 26 shows the production possibility curves of two countries each producing only two commodities. Country B is a much larger economy.

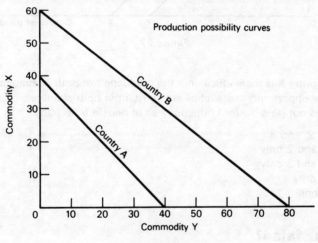

Figure 26

The diagram tells us, that

A   country B has an absolute advantage in the production of both commodities.
B   country A has a comparative advantage in the production of Y.
C   country B has a comparative advantage in the production of X.
D   none of the above statements is correct.

21 Figure 27 shows the production possibility boundaries (XX and YY) of two countries X and Y.

Which of the following statements is/are correct?
On the basis of the information in the diagram it can be said that

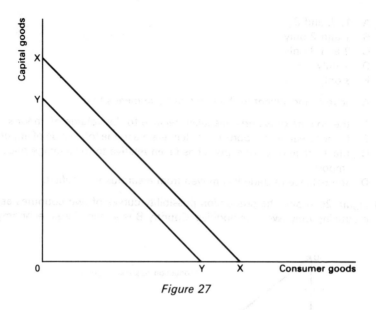

Figure 27

1   country X is more efficient in the production of both commodities.
2   the opportunity costs ratios are constant in both countries.
3   it is not possible for both countries to benefit from trade.

A   1, 2, and 3
B   1 and 2 only
C   2 and 3 only
D   1 only
E   3 only

True or false?

22 a International trade allows a country to consume beyond its production possibility curves.
b The theory of comparative costs holds that each country should specialise in supplying those goods which it can produce more cheaply than other countries.
c It is self-evident that low-wage countries have lower labour costs than high-wage countries.
d Even if country A is twice as efficient as country B in all economic activities, total output could still be increased if the countries specialised and traded.
e A country has a comparative advantage over a second country in the production of the commodity in which it has a higher opportunity cost than the other country.

f For a country to gain from international trade, the opportunity cost of obtaining goods through international trade must be less than the opportunity cost of producing them domestically.

Data response questions

23 Figure 28 refers to a single country which accounts for a very small part of the total world trade in commodity X. The line SS shows the supply of the country's import-competing industry and DD is the domestic consumers' demand curve for this commodity. Initially the country operates no barriers to international trade and the commodity is sold on the home market at world prices. PP is the supply curve of the rest of the world to this particular market.

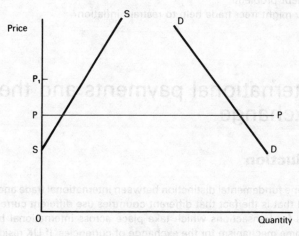

Figure 28

a Draw this diagram on your answer sheet and indicate
  (i) the quantities produced by the home industry,
  (ii) the quantity imported,
  (iii) the total domestic consumption.
b Now assume that the country imposes a tariff which raises the domestic price to OP₁. Insert the new world supply curve on your diagram and indicate
  (i) the output of the domestic industry,
  (ii) the quantity imported,
  (iii) the total domestic consumption,
  (iv) the total amount of import duties paid to the government.
c Use the diagram to discuss the impact of the tariff on total economic welfare.

24 This question is based on the following short quotations taken from an article on 'Protectionism' in the IMF and World Bank publication *Finance and Development*, March 1983.

'Protectionism is likely to lead to a misallocation of resources, to slow down the pace of necessary structural adjustment, and to invite retaliation in other countries.'

'Free and expanding trade is crucial for Third World development; it is needed urgently now to help some developing countries to overcome their debt problems.'

'Free trade fosters growth – and therefore jobs and higher incomes – and, at the same time, it tends to restrain inflation.'

a What is the nature of the *structural adjustment* referred to in the first quotation and in what sense is it necessary?
b How would free and expanding trade help developing countries with their debt problem?
c How might freer trade help to restrain inflation?

2 International payments and the rate of exchange

Introduction

There is one fundamental distinction between international trade and domestic trade and that is the fact that different countries use different currencies. The payments for transactions which take place across international boundaries require some mechanism for the exchange of currencies. If UK residents want to buy foreign goods and services they must be able to acquire foreign currencies, and similarly foreigners wanting to buy British commodities must be able to obtain sterling. This is the role of the foreign exchange market, and the rate at which one currency exchanges for another in this market is of vital importance for all major trading nations.

Since foreign goods and services must be paid for with foreign currencies, it follows that a nation's ability to buy abroad is determined by its ability to sell abroad (or to borrow abroad). For an open economy such as the UK (where foreign trade accounts for about 30 per cent of GNP), external financial relationships are a matter of great concern. The balance of payments tables present us with a summary of these financial relationships.

Short answer questions

25 Classify the following transactions according to the section of the balance of payments in which they appear:

  a UK residents' purchases of foreign cars,

  b US residents' purchases of shares in UK companies.

  c insurance of a French company's ships with Lloyds of London,

  d the receipts from foreign passengers using British Airways,

  e government expenditure on maintaining embassies abroad,

  f royalties paid by foreign firms using ICI patents,

  g a long-term loan from the UK to a developing country in Africa,

  h the repayment of an IMF loan by the UK.

26 The capital account in the balance of payments includes both *real investment and portfolio investment.* Distinguish between the terms in italics.

27 What is meant by the term 'hot money'?

28 Why is the *balancing item* in the balance of payments so named?

29 The figures in the UK balance of payments are recorded in pounds sterling. In what sense is this rather misleading?

30 Indicate the nature of the items which might appear under *Official Financing* when the overall balance of payments is in deficit.

31 The following figures are a summary of a country's balance of payments for a given year. The items are arranged in random order.

Visible exports	100
Private investment (net)	+80
Repayment of IMF loan	25
Visible imports	120
Official long-term capital (net)	−50
Changes in foreign-currency reserves	?
Invisible balance	+50
Balancing item	+30

Calculate

  a the current balance,

  b the balance for official financing,

  c the value and sign of the missing figure.

32 'A capital outflow resulting in real investment overseas will worsen the balance of payments. The longer-term effects of this transaction, however, will tend to be favourable.' Explain.

33 'For most of the twentieth century the British balance of payments on current account recorded a *deficit* on visible trade and a *surplus* on invisible trade, both of which could be explained by the principle of comparative advantage.' Explain.

34 Indicate the types of problem which might be created by countries running persistent surpluses.

35 When the exchange rates between currencies are fixed it is convenient and meaningful to express the value of a particular currency in terms of some major currency (e.g. the dollar). How can we measure changes in the value of a currency when all the major currencies are floating?

36 'Multilateral trade cannot really develop unless the major currencies are freely _____.' What is the missing word?

37 What do the advocates of fixed exchange rates see as the major advantages of the system?

38 Give two reasons why a freely floating exchange rate will not bring about an automatic and rapid adjustment to equilibrium when an economy is experiencing a surplus or deficit on its balance of payments.

39 'Under a system of fixed exchange rates the burden of a balance-of-payments deficit falls initially on the foreign currency reserves.' Explain.

40 Which of the following developments **a** increases the supply of pounds in the foreign exchange market, **b** increases the supply of dollars in the market?

(a) There is a large increase in the number of American tourists visiting Britain.

(b) The UK has to import large amounts of American capital equipment for use in the North Sea.

(c) The UK makes a large annual interest payment on an American loan.

41 Suppose that at a particular moment in time the exchange rates in a free market are

£1 = $2, $1 = 4 francs, £1 = 7.5 francs.

What type of speculative activity will take place and what will be the effects of this activity?

42 What effect does devaluation have on the burden of an overseas debt?

43 In describing the effects of devaluation on the balance of payments, economists often refer to the 'J-curve effect'. What is this effect?

44 One way of bringing about a short-term improvement in the balance of payments is to raise domestic rates of interest. Explain why this is so.

45 Which of the following would be described as *expenditure–switching* measures?

(a) Devaluation.

(b) The imposition of tariffs.

(c) Quotas.

(d) Deflationary measures.

Multiple choice questions

46 The Exchange Equalisation Account
1   controls the gold and foreign currency reserves of the UK.
2   sells pounds when the external value of the pound rises above some officially acceptable rate.
3   is managed by the Bank of England.

A   1, 2, and 3
B   1 and 2 only
C   2 and 3 only
D   1 only
E   3 only

47 The only two items in the official financing section of a particular country's balance of payments are:
Changes in foreign currency reserves -100
Transactions with the IMF -50
Which of the following statements is/are correct?
1   The country had a deficit on its balance of payments.
2   The country had a surplus on its balance of payments.
3   The foreign currency reserves fell by 100.
4   The country repaid a loan to the IMF.

A   1 only
B   1 and 3
C   2 and 4
D   1, 3, and 4

48 This question relates to Figure 29.

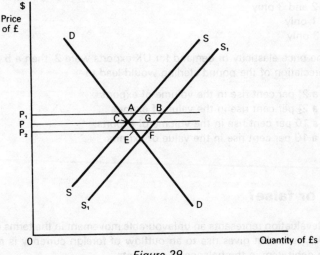

Figure 29

103

OP is the long-run equilibrium price of pounds in terms of dollars. The government wishes to maintain the value of the pound within the range OP_1 to OP_2. Now suppose a large increase in imports pushes the supply curve outwards to S_1S_1. The government will now be obliged to

A   buy AB pounds.
B   sell CG pounds.
C   buy EF pounds.
D   sell AB pounds.

49 This question refers to the following items.
1   Visible balance.
2   Invisible balance.
3   Investment and other capital flows.
4   Balancing item.
5   Current balance.
6   Balance for official financing.
Which of the following statements is *wrong*?

A $1 + 2 = 5$
B $1 + 2 + 3 + 4 = 6$
C $3 + 4 + 5 = 6$
D $1 + 2 + 4 = 5$

50 Revaluation would make
1   exports cheaper in terms of the domestic currency.
2   imports dearer in terms of foreign currency.
3   exports dearer in terms of foreign currency.

A   1, 2, and 3
B   1 and 2 only
C   2 and 3 only
D   1 only
E   3 only

51 If the price elasticity of demand for UK exports were 2, then a 5 per cent depreciation of the pound sterling would lead to

A   a $2\frac{1}{2}$ per cent rise in the volume of exports.
B   a $2\frac{1}{2}$ per cent rise in the value of exports.
C   a 10 per cent rise in the volume of exports.
D   a 10 per cent rise in the value of exports.

True or false?

52 a Revaluation represents an unfavourable movement in the terms of trade.
b Any item that gives rise to an outflow of foreign currency is recorded as a debit item in the balance of payments.

c World exports = world imports.

d In the balance of payments account, the export of capital is recorded as a debit item and the export of goods as a credit item.

e If, in managing the exchange rate, the authorities find that the foreign currency reserves continue to fall, the target rate is below the free market rate.

f Transactions in the forward exchange market are a form of 'hedging'.

g A country with a lower than average inflation rate benefits from a fixed exchange rate which insulates it from the effects of higher inflation rates in other countries.

Data response questions

53 The table below gives the summary accounts of the balance of payments for a country in two consecutive years.

	Year 1	Year 2
Visible trade		
Exports	500	480
Imports	520	460
Visible balance	−20	+20
Invisible trade (net)	+50	+50
Current balance	+30	+70
Investment and capital flows		
Long-term investment	−60	−20
Short-term investment	+40	−20
Total currency flow	+10	+30
Official financing		
Change in foreign currency reserves	−10	−30

Superficially the record for year 2 provides a more favourable picture than that for year 1. In fact the external financial relationships of this country had been deteriorating throughout year 1 and a serious deficit was avoided in year 2 by the application of a series of defensive measures. Explain what measures might have been taken and show how they might have affected the items in the table.

54 The following excerpts are taken from 'A Survey of the World Economy', *The Economist*, 24 September 1983.

'Fixed exchange rates collapsed unavoidably; floating was their least bad alternative, but it has introduced new and harmful uncertainties into business life. It has also produced unstable real exchange rates, a new and harmful cause of protectionism. Short of restoring fixed rates, what could make floating work better?'

'One argument is that intervention – central banks buying currencies that are weakening, selling those that are strengthening – can make exchange rates more stable. And, runs this argument, experience with such intervention has produced encouraging results over the past 10 years. Central banks have not given speculators a one-way bet, succumbing to pressure only after they have spent billions of dollars from their reserves.'

a What is meant by the term *real exchange rates*?

b Under what type of exchange rate system are speculators likely to be given the opportunity of making one-way bets? Explain your answer.

c What exactly would central banks have been trying to achieve in 'spending billions of dollars from their reserves'?

3 International cooperation

Introduction

In the years since the Second World War there has been an increasing awareness of the economic interdependence of countries. Few, if any, countries can 'go it alone' economically. Changes in the rate of economic growth, the rate of inflation, the rate of technical progress or the types of economic policies being pursued in any one of the major trading areas can have marked effects on economies elsewhere in the world.

Plans for a large measure of economic cooperation were already being prepared during the Second World War and since that time there has been an enormous growth in the extent and variety of international collaboration on economic matters. These economic groupings range from relatively loose arrangements such as some free-trade areas to closely integrated customs unions such as the EEC. Some associations such as the IMF, the World Bank, and the GATT are organised on a world-wide basis and embrace almost every country in the non-communist world, while others are relatively small economic units. Many of these trade agreements concern regional groupings such as the free-trade areas in South-East Asia, Latin America, and Africa. Some international agreements such as those governing the exports of wheat, oil, and coffee relate to a single product, while others such as the GATT are concerned with trade in a vast range of commodities.

Short answer questions

55 State, briefly, the main aims of the IMF (the International Monetary Fund).

56 'Technically members do not *borrow* from the IMF.' How then do they obtain assistance from the Fund?

57 'Since certainty is good for business confidence, Bretton Woods was a friend of the real economy.' To what features of the foreign exchange market does this quotation refer?

58 Most of the IMF's foreign-currency resources are provided by the subscriptions of member countries, but it also has a claim to resources which are not provided in this way. How are these additional resources obtained?

59 a What is meant by the term *international liquidity*?
b What are the components of international liquidity?
c Why is the total supply and distribution of international liquidity so important?

60 The financial resources of the Fund are now valued in SDRs. What are SDRs?

61 What are the major differences in structure between a free-trade area and a customs union?

62 What economic advantages of membership are common to both free-trade areas and customs unions?

63 How does the EEC Common Agricultural Policy (CAP) support EEC farmers?

64 What is the major item of expenditure of the CAP?

65 Distinguish between the role of the Commission and the role of the Council of Ministers in the EEC.

66 Once a customs union has eliminated all tariffs and quotas on trade between member countries, it is still faced with the difficult task of eliminating the many non-tariff barriers to trade. Give some examples of non-tariff barriers.

67 The IMF and the IBRD (the World Bank) are sister institutions. They were established at the same time and have the same membership. How do the two institutions differ: **a** in the form of assistance they provide, and **b** in the way they obtain their funds?

68 Identify the main sources and forms of aid available to developing countries.

69 'The less developed countries must receive foreign aid if they are to break out of the vicious circle of poverty.' What is this vicious circle?

70 Two basic principles of the General Agreement on Tariffs and Trade (GATT) are
(*a*) the principle of *non-discrimination in international trade*, and
(*b*) the principle of *reciprocity in tariff reductions*.
Explain what is meant by the terms in italics.

71 What are the main problems in operating an international buffer stock of a commodity as a means of stabilising its price in world markets?

Multiple choice questions

Questions **72–74** relate to the following international associations and organisations.

A OECD
B GAB
C IDA
D ECSC

Which of the above

72 exists to supplement the resources of the IMF?

73 is an affiliate of the World Bank?

74 is a common market?

75 The European Community Budget is financed by member states which must pay over to the community
  1 customs duties on imports of goods subject to the common external tariff.
  2 agricultural import levies.
  3 VAT up to 1 per cent of a standardised tax base.

A 1, 2, and 3
B 1 and 2 only
C 2 and 3 only
D 1 only
E 3 only

True or false?

76 a When a nation repurchases its own currency from the IMF it automatically increases its drawing rights.
  b An issue of SDRs represents a genuine increase in international liquidity.
  c Strictly speaking the formation of a customs union infringes the basic principles of the GATT.
  d World Bank loans are restricted to governments and publicly-owned enterprises.
  e EFTA and EEC now comprise a single free-trade area in industrial goods.

Data response question

77 The data below show the cost situations in three countries each producing two commodities which are traded internationally. Countries A and C are about to form a customs union. Each country operates a 50 per cent *ad valorem* tariff on imports, but after the formation of the union, this tariff will only apply to exports from country B. In the light of the data given, examine the effects of the creation of the customs union **a** in respect of *trade diversion*, and **b** in respect of *trade creation*. Ignore transport costs.

Country A

	Cost per unit
Commodity X	20
Commodity Y	16

Country B

	Cost per unit
Commodity X	12
Commodity Y	14

Country C

	Cost per unit
Commodity X	15
Commodity Y	13

Part 10
Public finance

Introduction

This section is concerned with the way a society deals with problems of satisfying *collective* wants and with the economic problems associated with the government or public sector of the economy. In most countries the public sector accounts for a relatively large part of the total economy. In the UK, for example, total public expenditure in 1983 amounted to about 45 per cent of the gross national product.

Economists are interested in such matters as the division of resources between the public and private sectors; the division of resources within the public sector; the economic effects of public expenditures; and the economic effects of diverting resources from private to public use (i.e. taxation and borrowing). Government expenditure and taxation profoundly influence all the important macro-economic variables (output, employment, prices, the rate of growth, the rate of exchange, and so on) and the Budget itself is the major instrument of economic policy (although many economists now believe that the regulation of the money supply is more important).

Short answer questions

1 Most of the government income and expenditure in the UK flows into and out of two major funds.
  a What are these funds?
  b What is the main distinction between them?

2 The following list is a very broad classification of the functions of public finance:
  (*a*) to provide public goods and services;
  (*b*) to regulate economic activities;
  (*c*) to influence resource allocation and economic efficiency;
  (*d*) to achieve important social objectives;
  (*e*) to influence the level of economic activity.
  Provide one or two examples of government activities in each of these areas of economic policy.

3 What institutions are included in *the public sector* of the economy?

4 Total public spending in the UK accounts for about 45 per cent of the GNP, but the share of the national product directly pre-empted by the state is only about 27 per cent of the GNP. Explain the reason for the difference in these proportions.

5 'Over the fairly short period a large part of public expenditure is not directly under the control of the government; it is demand-determined.' Explain this statement giving examples of the types of public expenditure to which it refers.

6 Almost 90 per cent of the total revenue from taxation is derived from seven major taxes. Name these taxes.

7 What major source of government income does not appear in the Budget statement although it is in fact a form of direct taxation?

8 Indicate **a** the main categories of holders of the UK national debt, and **b** the main forms in which the debt is held.

9 The absolute size of the UK national debt has increased enormously over the past fifty years, yet we are told that the 'burden' of the debt has actually diminished. What is the explanation for this apparent paradox?

10 'Indexation will combine with demography to produce a growing social security burden for the rest of society.'
Explain the nature of the linkages between demographic change, indexation, and the social security burden.

11 Taxes are usually classified as progressive, proportional, or regressive. To which category do **a**, **b** and **c** belong?

Taxable income (£)	Amount paid in tax (£)		
	a	b	c
2000	200	200	200
3000	300	270	360
4000	400	320	600
5000	500	350	1000
6000	600	360	1500

12 Can economic theory provide any support for the view that a progressive income tax is the most equitable type of taxation?

13 An important objective of fiscal policy is to bring about a more equal distribution of income and wealth. To this end the state provides various social benefits which may be classified as (*a*) benefits in cash; (*b*) benefits in kind; and (*c*) indirect benefits.
Give examples of each type of benefit.

14 **a** What do we mean by the *incidence* of a tax?
b Where does the incidence of (i) an income tax, (ii) an expenditure or outlay tax, fall?

15 How does the Public Sector Borrowing Requirement (ᴾSBR) differ from the Central Government's Borrowing Requirement (CGBR)?

16 How might a large and increasing PSBR affect **a** the rate of interest, and **b** the money supply?

17 One feature of the British system of public finance which has been given increasing publicity in recent years is the so-called *poverty trap*. What exactly is meant by this term?

Multiple choice questions

Questions **18**, **19**, and **20** refer to Figure 30 which shows the effect of a government granting a subsidy to producers of a product.

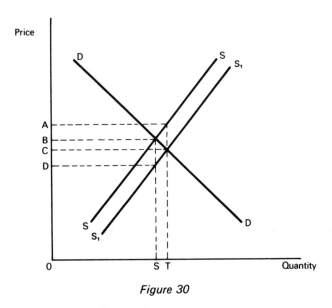

Figure 30

18 What is the market price after the introduction of the subsidy?

    A   0A
    B   0B
    C   0C
    D   0D

19 Including the payment of the subsidy, how much do producers receive for each unit sold?

    A   0A
    B   0B
    C   0C
    D   0D

20 What is the total cost to the government of this subsidy?

    A   BD × 0S
    B   BC × 0S
    C   0C × 0T
    D   AC × 0T

21 Which of the following items constitute part of the National Debt?
1   Treasury bills
2   National Savings Certificates
3   Premium Bonds

A   1, 2, and 3
B   1 and 2 only
C   2 and 3 only
D   1 only
E   3 only

22 A country with unemployed resources plans a substantial Budget deficit by leaving tax rates unchanged and significantly increasing government spending. Which of the following are likely effects of this policy?
1   An increase in national income.
2   A fall in the numbers unemployed.
3   An increase in tax revenues.

A   1, 2, and 3
B   1 and 2 only
C   2 and 3 only
D   1 only
E   3 only

23 Increased government expenditure on goods and services financed by long-term borrowing
1   transfers the real burden of the expenditure to future generations.
2   is likely to increase the National Debt.
3   will probably lead to an increase in tax revenues.

Which of the above statements is correct?

A   1, 2, and 3
B   1 and 2 only
C   2 and 3 only
D   1 only
E   3 only

24 Which of the following changes would be classified as fiscal measures?
1   An increase in VAT.
2   A planned reduction in government borrowing.
3   A cut in investment grants to industry.

A   1, 2, and 3
B   1 and 2 only
C   2 and 3 only
D   1 only
E   3 only

True or false?

25 a Subsidies which are intended to hold down the cost of living would be most effective when applied to goods with inelastic demands.

b A reduction in income taxes and an increase in indirect taxes would make the tax system in the UK less regressive.

c If the marginal rate of taxation is higher than the average rate, the tax is described as progressive.

d Other things being equal, a large increase in the size of a Budget deficit will probably lead to an increase in interest rates.

e Social security benefits make up the largest single item of expenditure in the UK Budget.

f Fiscal measures which transfer income from people with high MPCs to people with low MPCs will tend to increase aggregate demand.

Data response questions

26 This question is based on two different schemes for the taxation of personal income

Scheme A

The personal allowance (i.e. income not subject to tax) is £4000 per annum. Taxable income is subject to tax at the following rates.

Taxable income (£s)	Rate of tax (per cent)
0–3000	10
3001–4000	15
4001–5000	20
5001–6000	25
6001–7000	30
7001–8000	35
8001–9000	40
9001–10000	45
10001–11000	50
11001–12000	55
12001+	60

Scheme B

The personal allowance is £7000 per annum and all taxable income is taxed at the single rate of 35 per cent.

a Prepare two graphs, one showing the marginal rates of taxation against *gross income* for both schemes, and the other showing average rates of taxation against gross income for both schemes.

b Comment on any differences between the two schemes in respect of their effects on incentives and on the distribution of income.

27 This question is based on the following extracts from the *Financial State-ment and Budget Report*, 1984–5.

'The growth of Government revenues in cash terms over the medium term will depend on the growth of incomes, spending and prices, as well as policy decisions. Revenue is projected on the conventional assumption of constant tax rates and indexed allowances and thresholds at the proposed 1984–85 levels, except where the Budget contains specific proposals for changes in the later years. All changes proposed in the Budget are taken into account. No change is assumed in National Insurance contribution rates. Projections of North Sea tax revenues assume that oil prices do not change much from current levels for the next two years and then rise broadly in line with world inflation.'

General Government Receipts

£ billion, cash

	1982–83	1983–84	1984–85	1985–86	1986–87	1987–88	1988–89
Taxes on incomes expenditure and capital	92.4	96½	104½	111½	119½	126	132
National Insurance and other contributions	18.7	21½	23	24½	26	27½	29
Interest and other receipts	11.1	10½	10	10½	11	11½	11½
Accruals adjustment	−0.1	—	+1	−½	−½	−½	−½
Total	**122.1**	**128½**	**138½**	**146½**	**156½**	**164½**	**172**
of which North Sea tax(¹)	7.8	9	10	9½	9½	9½	9

(¹) Royalties, petroleum revenue tax (including advance payments), corporation tax from North Sea Sea oil and gas production (before advance corporation tax set off) and, in 1982–83, supplementary petroleum duty.

Constituent items may not sum to totals due to rounding to nearest £½ billion.

a Why is it necessary to distinguish between changes in prices and changes in spending as influences on government revenues?
b Explain what is meant by '... indexed allowances and thresholds at the proposed 1984–85 levels'.
c How can the information in the last sentence of the quotation be reconciled with the figures in the table?

Part 11
Managing the economy

1 The economy as a whole

Introduction

The overall performance of the economy is now accepted as a major, probably *the* major, responsibility of government. In this section we look at the problems of formulating and implementing economic policies designed to influence the national levels of output, employment, the general level of prices, the rate of economic growth, and the balance of payments. All these are part of the subject matter of macro-economics (the study of the behaviour of economic aggregates). But the formulation of policy presupposes a knowledge of how the economy works and we begin with questions about the workings of a fairly simple model of the mixed economy.

In this section some use is made of the following abbreviations.

Y = national income C = consumption S = saving I = investment
G = government spending on goods and services X = exports M = imports
T = taxation.

Short answer questions

Questions **1** to **10** refer to an economy in which there are only two sectors, households and firms.

1 Identify the various flows, both real and monetary, between households and firms.

2 Define the terms *leakages* (or *withdrawals*) and *injections* in relation to the circular flow of income.

3 Consumption rises less-than-proportionately as income rises. What, then, happens to the marginal propensity to consume (MPC) and the marginal propensity to save (MPS) as income rises?

Questions **4** to **7** refer to Figure 31 which shows expenditure plotted against income for the economy as a whole. Since the scales on both axes are the same, the 45° line shows all points where income is equal to expenditure. The CC line shows the level of consumption at each level of income.

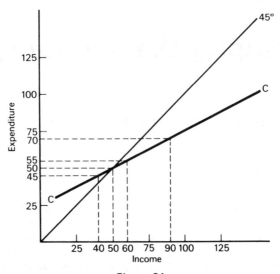

Figure 31

4 In Figure 31, MPC is constant. What is its value?

5 What is the value of the average propensity to consume (APC) when income is 40?

6 What is the amount of saving when income is 60?

7 If investment is constant at 20, what is the equilibrium level of income?

8 a One of the most puzzling features of the theory of the circular flow of income is the statement that 'realised' investment is always equal to 'realised' saving. How do we define S and I so tht $S \equiv I$?
b The following table shows the values of the macro-economic variables in a given time period.

Total output = total income = 100
Consumption   = 70
Saving   = 30
Planned investment   = 20

In this particular time period, what was the value of realised investment? Explain your answer.

9 An economy is in equilibrium. Households now decide to increase the proportion of income saved (i.e. the APS). If other things remain equal, what will happen to the levels of income and saving?

10 In a two-sector economy, MPC = 0.8.
   a What is the value of the multiplier?
   b Investment now increases by £10000. What will be the values of the

next three terms in the following series (which result from the increase in *I*)?

Increase in income = £10 000 + ? + ? + ? + ...

Increase in saving = £2000 + ? + ? + ? + ...

c What is the value of the eventual increase in income?

Questions **11** to **19** refer to an open economy with government (i.e. a four-sector economy).

11 What items make up **a** the leakages, and **b** the injections, in this type of economy?

12 There are two ways of expressing the value of the multiplier in this type of economy.

(i) Multiplier = $\dfrac{1}{\text{marginal rate of ?}}$

(iii) Multiplier = $\dfrac{1}{? + ? + ?}$

a What is the missing word in (i)?
b What are the missing terms in (ii)?

13 Of every extra £1 of national income, a community saves 15p, spends 10p on foreign goods and services, and the government takes 20p in taxation. What is the value of the multiplier?

14 Two different equations may be used to express the conditions necessary for an equilibrium level of income in a four-sector economy. What are they?

15 This question refers to the following planned leakages and injections in an economy.

	£ million
Government spending on goods and services	80
Taxes	90
Exports	50
Saving	80
Investment	70

There is one item missing. What is it and what value must it have to produce an equilibrium level of income?

Questions **16** and **17** refer to Figure 32 where AD represents the aggregate demand schedule and 0F represents the full employment level of income at the existing price level.

16 What does the amount ab represent?

17 In order to achieve full employment, the government decides to increase its own expenditures on goods and services.
a By how much must government spending be increased?
b What is the value of the multiplier which will apply to this increase in government spending?

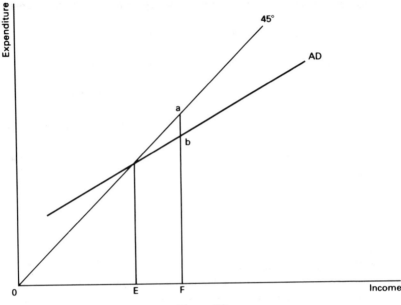

Figure 32

18 Monetarists contend that there is a stable and predictable relationship between the rate of growth of the money supply and the rate of growth of money national income.
a What assumptions does this theory make about the behaviour of *V* (the velocity of circulation of money)?
b On the basis of the relationship outlined above, explain how a strict control of the money supply might lead to labour 'pricing itself out of jobs.'

19 Keynesian theory indicates that relatively high levels of unemployment might be reduced by measures which increase aggregate demand. Many economists, however, now believe that measures to stimulate demand are likely to affect prices rather than output, even when the economy has a large amount of excess capacity. What is the basis for this argument?

Multiple choice questions

20 An increase in investment of £10 million sets up a series of increments in total spending as follows:

£10m. + £6m. + £3.6m. + ... + ... + ...

The value of the multiplier is

A 0.6   C 2.5
B 1.66   D 5.0

Questions **21**, **22**, and **23** are based on Figure 33 which shows the C and (C + I) schedules for a closed economy with no government.

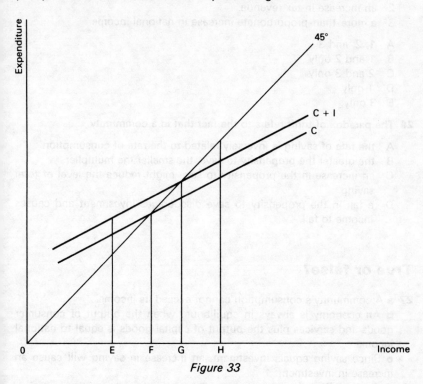

Figure 33

From the income levels shown below, select the one, if any, which satisfies the conditions set out in questions **21** to **23**.

    A 0E
    B 0F
    C 0G
    D 0H
    E Cannot be determined from the information provided.

21 Planned saving is zero.

22 The full employment level of income.

23 Planned saving equals planned investment.

24 In an economy the marginal rates of leakage are constant and $T = 0.2Y$, $C = 0.75$ of disposable income, and $M = 0.25C$. The proportion of income saved is

    A 0.05Y   C 0.25Y
    B 0.2Y   *D* 0.4Y

121

25 Other things being equal, an increase in exports will lead to

1 an increase in the level of saving.
2 an increase in tax revenue.
3 a more-than-proportionate increase in national income.

A 1, 2, and 3
B 1 and 2 only
C 2 and 3 only
D 1 only
E 3 only

26 The paradox of thrift refers to the fact that in a community

A the rate of saving is inversely related to the rate of consumption.
B the greater the propensity to save, the smaller the multiplier.
C an increase in the propensity to save might reduce the level of total saving.
D a fall in the propensity to save discourages investment and causes income to fall.

True or false?

27 a A community's consumption cannot exceed its income.

b An economy is always in equilibrium when the output of consumer goods and services plus the output of capital goods is equal to national income.

c Since saving equals investment, an increase in saving will cause an increase in investment.

d A fall in the propensity to save will increase the value of the multiplier.

e An increase in exports will reduce the national income because more goods and services are leaving the country.

f An economy may be in equilibrium even when it is running a Budget deficit.

g In the circular flow of income, the larger the proportion of income passed on, the greater is the change in income for any given change in aggregate expenditure.

h The value of the multiplier is equal to the reciprocal of the fraction of income not passed on.

Data response question

28 In a three-sector economy (i.e. firms, households, and government, no foreign trade), MPC and APC are constant and equal to 0.75 of *disposable income*. Investment expenditure is constant at £1000 million.

a What is meant by disposable income?

b Assume initially that there is no government activity. What is the equilibrium level of national income?
c Now assume that the government introduces a tax equal to 20 per cent of income.
(i) What is the value of the multiplier?
(ii) What is the new equilibrium level of income?
d If the government now decides to introduce public expenditure equal to £1000 million, what will be the new equilibrium level of income?

2 Economic policies

Introduction

There is a fairly wide measure of political agreement on the aims of economic policy, but considerable disagreement on the means of achieving these aims and upon the priorities accorded to them. The major objectives of economic policy may be summarised as follows:

(a) a high and stable level of employment,
(b) price stability,
(c) a satisfactory balance of payments position,
(d) a politically acceptable rate of economic growth,
(e) a more equitable distribution of income and wealth.

Governments have found that some of these objectives may be incompatible. For example, policies designed to achieve full employment may be successful, but the 'costs' of these policies may be a high rate of inflation and a serious balance-of-payments deficit. This means that political decisions have to be taken on questions of priorities.

In this and the following sections, the questions are based on the objectives of government economic policy, the various measures used to achieve those objectives, and the ways in which these measures operate on the macro-economic variables such as employment, output, prices, exports, imports, and so on. An appreciation of the workings of the circular flow of income model is necessary if we are to understand how policy measures are likely to affect the economy.

A   Full employment

Short answer questions

29 The following rates of unemployment are experienced by two different countries:

	Country A	Country B
Year 1	3%	5%
Year 2	3%	1%
Year 3	3%	4%
Year 4	3%	1%
Year 5	3%	4%
Average	3%	3%

Should the employment policies in these two countries be regarded as equally successful?

30 A country is suffering from cyclical unemployment and it is estimated that national income is some £10 000 million below the figure required to produce a full employment level of income. The MPC of the community is 0.75.

a Assuming that other things remain equal, by how much must aggregate demand be increased in order to achieve a full employment level of income?

b In the 1960s and 1970s attempts to achieve full employment by increasing aggregate demand had to be abandoned before their objective was achieved. What developments caused governments (temporarily?) to drop the full employment objective?

31 In most developed countries fiscal policy contains some measures which act automatically; they are described as 'built-in stabilisers'.
Give some examples of built-in stabilisers.

32 Why is a straightforward increase in aggregate demand not likely to be a very effective method of dealing with frictional unemployment?

33 Why are measures designed to increase the mobility of labour an essential ingredient of a full employment policy?

34 'Each extra 100 000 unemployment cost the Treasury about £438 million in 1981–2.' Itemise the various components in the total cost figure.

35 How would you account for the fact that while over the period 1974–81, real GDP in the UK rose on average by about 0.25 per cent per annum, over the same period, unemployment more than doubled?

36 Why is the use of investment grants as a means of reducing unemployment in the development areas criticised as being a very expensive way of creating jobs?

37 Why is the natural rate of unemployment sometimes referred to as the non-accelerating inflation rate of unemployment?

Multiple choice questions

38 The question is based on Figure 34 which shows the market supply and demand curves for a particular occupation.

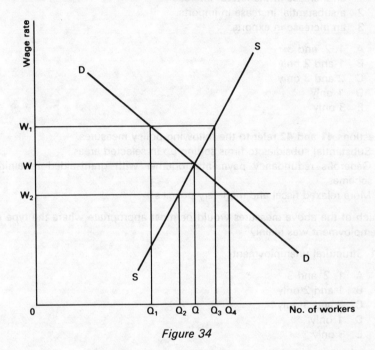

Figure 34

If the goverment imposes both a minimum wage rate of $0W_2$ and a maximum wage rate of $0W_1$, which of the following will result? (Assume competitive conditions in the labour market.)

A   Employment will fall from $0Q_4$ to $0Q_1$.
B   Employment will fall from $0Q$ to $0Q_1$.
C   There will be an excess supply of labour equal to $0Q_1-0Q_3$.
D   The wage rate and the numbers employed will remain unchanged.

39 Which of the following would be desirable if there were large-scale unemployment?
1   A Budget deficit.
2   A fall in interest rates.
3   An increase in exports.

A 1, 2, and 3
B 1 and 2 only
C 2 and 3 only
D 1 only
E 3 only

40 Governments' attempts to reduce unemployment by increasing aggregate demand will be rendered less effective if, at the same time, there is
1 an increase in the rate of interest.
2 a substantial increase in imports.
3 an increase in exports.

A 1, 2, and 3
B 1 and 2 only
C 2 and 3 only
D 1 only
E 3 only

Questions **41** and **42** refer to the following policy measures.
1 Substantial subsidies to firms setting up in selected areas.
2 Generous redundancy payments together with grant-aided retraining schemes.
3 More relaxed fiscal and monetary policies.

Which of the above measures would be most appropriate where the type of unemployment was mainly

41 Structural unemployment?

A 1, 2, and 3
B 1 and 2 only
C 2 and 3 only
D 1 only
E 3 only

42 Cyclical (or deficient-demand) unemployment?

A 1, 2, and 3
B 1 and 2 only
C 2 and 3 only
D 1 only
E 3 only

True or false?

43 a The official UK unemployment figures tell us the total number of people who are willing to undertake paid employment but cannot find a job.
b If over an extended period of time it is found that the great majority

of those on the unemployment register have only been out of work for
a few weeks, the problem is one of frictional unemployment.
c A stable level of aggregate demand means a stable level of employment.
d The operation of unrestricted market forces will always tend to move
a capitalist system to a full-employment equilibrium.

Data response question

44 This question is based on the following table.

Changes in employment*,
GB

	Employees 000s			Change 1973–83	
	June 1973	June 1979	June 1983	No. 000s	% per annum
All industries and services	22180	22590	20460	−1720	−0.8
Agriculture, forestry and fishing	420	360	340	−80	−2.1
Mining and quarrying	360	350	310	−50	−1.5
Manufacturing	7660	7050	5370	−2290	−3.5
Construction	1340	1250	970	−370	−3.2
Gas, electricity and water	340	340	320	−20	−0.4
Services industries	12060	13240	13150	+1090	+0.9

* (i) Figures are based on 1968 Standard Industrial Classification. (Figures on 1980 SIC basis
are not yet available.)
(ii) The 1983 figures are the Department of Employment's supplementary series which includes
an allowance for the probable understatement of the level of employment, particularly in the
service industries, in the basic series.
(iii) The 1983 figures do not reflect the final results of the 1981 Census of Employment.
(Source: *Economic Progress Report 165*, February 1984.)

What are the main factors accounting for the substantial changes in the
relative importance of the manufacturing and service sectors as employers
of labour?

B Inflation

Short answer questions

45 'Faced with a situation where there is excess demand, the government
may wish to curb private investment. Since saving is always equal to investment the government can reduce investment by lowering interest
rates in order to discourage saving.'
What flaws can you find in this reasoning?

46 a Why may a rise in interest rates prove an ineffective deterrent to borrowers during demand inflation?
b If a large increase in the rate of interest does succeed in reducing the demand for loans, what are the longer-term disadvantages?

47 'A reduction in the money supply may not bring about any immediate fall in aggregate demand. By making changes in their business and financial practices, people can, for a time at least, offset the effects of a fall in the money supply.' To what kind of changes does this quotation refer?

48 a What developments might initiate a rise in the general price level independently of the level of demand in the home economy?
b What factors might then cause this rise in prices to develop into an inflationary spiral?

49 'Two ways of squeezing inflation another point or so – thinner profit margins and a rising pound – would stop Britain's recovery in its tracks.' Explain why the two suggested measures **a** are anti-inflationary, and **b** would inhibit recovery.

50 'When oil prices were quadrupled in 1973–4 and more than doubled in 1979–80, the effects were deflationary in terms of demand and inflationary in terms of the ripple effect created on prices generally.' Explain briefly how the deflationary and inflationary effects came about.

51 'In this view, trade unions "cause" inflation only to the extent that they successfully induce governments to passively adjust the_____ _____ to offset what would otherwise be the unemployment consequences of excessive wage claims.'
a What are the missing words?
b In the context of the quotation, what is meant by 'excessive wage claims'?

52 'When inflation was falling in 1981–3, the opportunity cost of keeping money in the more convenient current accounts was reduced. As a result the M1 measure of the money supply tended to rise faster than £M3.'
a Why did the opportunity cost of keeping money in current accounts fall?
b What caused M1 to grow faster than £M3?

53 Many people believe that the problems of inflation can be overcome by a rigid system of price controls. What are the main economic disadvantages of such a policy?

54 a What is the *main* objective of an incomes policy?
b Explain briefly, using simple supply and demand analysis, how an incomes policy is intended to achieve its main objective.

Multiple choice questions

55 In a fully employed economy, other things being equal, an increase in exports will be

A deflationary because more goods are leaving the country.

B deflationary because there will be a fall in home demand.

C inflationary because home supplies fall relative to demand.

D neutral because supply and demand both fall to the same extent.

56 Which of the following would have a part to play in a package of deflationary measures?

1 Open-market sales of securities by the central bank.

2 An increase in National Insurance contributions.

3 Subsidies on goods with inelastic demands.

A 1, 2, and 3

B 1 and 2

C 2 and 3

D 1 only

E 3 only

57 Which of the following measures is/are likely to initiate cost-push inflation?

1 A depreciation of the home currency in the foreign-exchange market.

2 A substantial increase in indirect taxes.

3 The removal of the subsidies on foodstuffs.

A 1, 2, and 3

B 1 and 2

C 2 and 3

D 1 only

E 3 only

58 In a fully employed economy, which of the following is/are likely to lead to demand-pull inflation?

1 A substantial budget deficit.

2 An increased export surplus.

3 Severe restrictions on imports.

A 1, 2, and 3

B 1 and 2

C 2 and 3

D 1 only

E 3 only

True or false?

59 a Cost-push inflation can only occur in conditions of full employment.

b Inflation cannot occur if the Budget is balanced.

c Since it will lead to an increase in prices, an increase in indirect taxation must always be inflationary.

d A major but formidable objective of an anti-inflationary policy is to bring about a change in workers' and consumers' expectations.

e The government must tackle inflation because increases in prices, whatever the causes, always lead to reductions in demand.

f Indexation is an attempt to make real incomes independent of inflation.

Data response question

60 This question is based on the following quotation.

'Economists have generally drawn a distinction between anticipated inflation which is fully taken account of in all economic transactions, and unanticipated inflation. Where inflation is fully anticipated then the costs of inflation are normally considered trivial.

'The reason why economists have worried about inflation is that it is generally unanticipated inflation which has effects on the distribution of income and wealth.

'One of these effects is a redistribution of income away from the private sector towards the government.'

a How may anticipated inflation be taken account of in economic transactions?

b Indicate two ways in which unanticipated inflation may lead to a redistribution of income away from the private sector to the government sector.

C The balance of payments

Short answer questions

61 'The UK's membership of international organisations places some restrictions on its freedom of action to use policies which act on the balance of payments.'

To which organisations does this quotation refer?

62 When a country is operating under a system of fixed exchange rates,

a why must the authorities maintain an adequate supply of foreign currencies?

b how might they supplement such reserves at short notice?

63 'Measures which reduce aggregate demand will tend to reduce a balance-of-payments deficit although they might give rise to *unfavourable feed-back effects from abroad.'*
Explain the terms in italics.

64 If a relatively small proportion of income is spent on imports, why would the use of expenditure-reducing measures to deal with a balance-of-payments deficit tend to be politically unpopular?

65 A country operating a fixed exchange rate has (*a*) unemployed resources, and (*b*) a serious balance-of-payments deficit. It wishes to avoid further devaluations of its currency. This raises serious problems with regard to the use of monetary policy because
a to improve the employment situation it should *raise/lower* interest rates; and
b to improve the balance-of-payments position it should *raise/lower* interest rates.
Choose the correct words from the pairs of words in italics.

66 A country's domestic currency is sterling. Its existing balance-of-payments position (expressed in foreign currency) is as follows:
    Exports $10 000   Imports $11 000.
The elasticity of demand for its exports = 2. Its elasticity of demand for imports = 1. The supplies of exports and imports are perfectly elastic. The country now devalues by 5 per cent.
a What will be the balance-of-payments position after the effects of devaluation have worked themselves out (assume other things remain equal)?
b What would be the likely effects on this situation if the supply of exports were inelastic?
c Faced with the situation in **b**, what might the government do in order to make the supply of exports more elastic?

67 When used to deal with balance-of-payments problems, which of the following might be described as expenditure-switching measures?
(*a*) Devaluation.
(*b*) The use of tariffs.
(*c*) The use of quotas.
(*d*) An increase in direct taxes.
(*e*) A rise in interest rates.

68 Comment briefly on the impact of North Sea oil on the UK economy in respect of
a the level of employment,
b the government's revenue,
c the balance of payments.

69 What is meant by the term *effective exchange rate*?

Multiple choice questions

70 Which of the following is/are likely to halt or reduce an inflow of 'hot money' into country X?
1 A fall in country X's domestic interest rates.
2 A threatened revaluation of country X's currency.
3 A growing balance-of-payments surplus in country X.

A 1, 2, and 3
B 1 and 2
C 2 and 3
D 1 only
E 3 only

71 Which of the following organisations or agreements exists in order to render short-term assistance to countries in balance-of-payments difficulties?

A IBRD
B GAB
C NEB
D IDA

72 Which of the following is *not* true of a tariff which effectively protects a domestic industry from foreign competition?

A It might provoke retaliation.
B It tends to reduce the pressures for more efficient home production.
C It yields a large revenue for the government.
D It infringes the basic principles of GATT.

73 Which of the following represents a favourable movement in the terms of trade?
1 An appreciation of sterling in terms of other currencies.
2 Inflation at home causing UK export prices to rise faster than world prices in general.
3 A favourable movement in the balance of trade.

A 1, 2, and 3
B 1 and 2 only
C 2 and 3 only
D 1 only
E 3 only

True or false?

74 a Other things being equal, revaluation would tend to reduce cost-push pressures.
b International reserves of foreign currency can only be increased if some countries are prepared to accept balance-of-payments deficits.
c Since an economy is only in equilibrium when leakages = injections, equilibrium requires that exports = imports.
d When a country devalues, it improves its terms of trade.
e When the pound is allowed to float downwards, the burden of the UK's overseas debt is reduced.
f Restricting imports from low-wage countries would help to force up wages in those countries.

Data response question

75 This question is based on the following short extracts from an article entitled 'The Role of the Exchange Rate' in the *Bank of England Quarterly Bulletin*, December 1983.

(i) 'Another source of major changes in the relationship between exchange rates can lie in the political perceptions of differing degrees of risk to private wealth; much of the inflow into the dollar in recent months has been ascribed to this "safe haven" motive.'
(ii) 'The *peaks of sterling and the dollar* have owed much to the *high* nominal and real *interest rates* associated with using *monetary discipline* to quell inflation.'
(iii) 'Perhaps the most harmful effect of all is the increased pressures for protection by producers in those countries whose exchange rates are currently overvalued in relation to some longer-run norm.'

Taking each quotation in turn,
a From what kind of dangers or risks did the dollar provide a 'safe haven'?
b Explain, briefly, the relationships between the terms in italics.
c Why should an overvalued currency lead to demands for protection?

D Economic growth

Short answer questions

76 Figure 35 shows the changes in potential national output achieved by a country over a period of years.

a Explain clearly the difference between a movement from A to B and a movement from B to C.
b Which of these movements is described as economic growth?

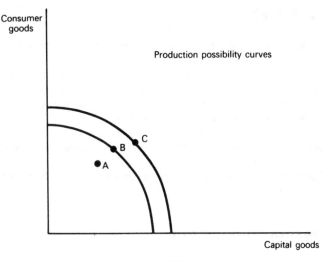

Figure 35

77 Which measurement of economic growth is most relevant to a discussion on standards of living?

78 Why does real income per person tend to grow more slowly than an economy's productive capacity per person?

79 Why is economic growth desirable from a government's point of view?

80 'Quite a modest rate of economic growth, if sustained, would mean that a man might quadruple his material standard of living in a working lifetime (i.e. 50 years).'
To what annual rate (approximate) of economic growth does this quotation refer?

81 'Even if the poor countries achieve the same growth rates as the richer countries, the gap between them will continue to widen.' Explain.

82 'Economic growth is dependent upon capital-deepening rather than capital-widening.' Explain.

83 *List* the main factors which influence the rate of economic growth.

84 Why might the people in a fully employed economy be reluctant to support an economic policy which aimed to achieve a much higher rate of economic growth?

85 Explain why, in the UK, attempts to speed up the rate of economic growth have appeared to come into conflict with the objectives of: **a** price stability; and **b** an equilibrium balance of payments.

86 In the 1970s investment in the UK was equal to about 18.7 per cent of GDP; in Japan it was more than 30 per cent. Productivity growth in Japan during the same period was much faster than in the UK. Does this prove that more investment means faster economic growth?

Multiple choice questions

87 In measuring economic growth we should include any increase in
1   the money supply.
2   the output of consumer goods and capital goods.
3   the value of shares.
4   the output of services.
5   the output of government-produced goods/services.

A   1, 2, and 3
B   1, 3, and 4
C   1, 4 and 5
D   2, 3, and 5
E   2, 4, and 5

88 Which of the following is the most acceptable measure of economic growth (assume all measurements are at constant prices)?

A   Changes in GNP per person employed per annum.
B   Changes in consumption per head per annum.
C   Changes in GNP per capita per annum.
D   Changes in national income per person employed per annum.

89 Throughout the nineteenth century the per capita growth rate in Britain averaged

A   less than 1 per cent.
B   between 1½ and 2 per cent.
C   between 3 and 5 per cent.
D   more than 5 per cent.

True or false?

90 a About 20 per cent of the world's peoples enjoy more than half of the world's real income.
b An underdeveloped country is one where population is growing faster than aggregate real income.
c The absence of a reasonably well-developed infrastructure is a major barrier to economic development.
d The expression 'invest now, consume later' draws attention to the opportunity costs of programmes designed to speed up the rate of economic growth.
e In the more developed countries technological progress has made a contribution to economic growth which is at least as important as that made by the growth of the stock of capital.
f A rapid rate of growth can only be sustained if there is a high degree of mobility in the labour force.

Data response question

91 'Economic development theory recognises the use of leading sectors as engines for growth. In our lifetimes we have seen examples of this theory in the automotive sector with its corollary of highway construction, and in armaments. Both of these have proven their capacity to mobilise resources on a broad scale – financial, material, and human – and to create a major multiplier effect on other sectors of the national economies.

'The two main conditions for the introduction of a leading sector of growth are a great latent demand and the capacity to mobilise internal resources to meet that demand.

'The construction and housing industries are the only major sectors in the developing economies for which all the basic materials, at least for traditional designs, are available nationally and for which there is no heavy import component.

'These industries also have a very high component of unskilled workers which cannot be absorbed in any other way without costly programmes of education and training. Thus, very large numbers of otherwise unusable labourers can be turned from a social liability to important economic contributors, as producers and then as consumers.'

(Extracted from 'The Need For A New Development Model', E. Penalosa, in *Finance and Development*, IMF and World Bank, Vol. 13; No. 1.)

a Explain the meaning of the term 'engines for growth' and the associated reference to the multiplier effect.

b Why does the article stress the fact that 'there is no heavy import content'?

c Why is the multiplier effect of an expansion of the construction industries likely to be particularly high?

d Can you think of other advantages (to a developing country) of these proposals?

E Inequalities of income and wealth

Short answer questions

92 How would you explain the fact that the inequality in the distribution of income is much greater in poor countries than in rich countries?

93 Why is the distribution of wealth much more unequal than the distribution of income?

94 Why has the inequality in the distribution of personal wealth in the UK lessened during this century?

95 The Royal Commission on the Distribution of Income and Wealth (1975) distinguished between marketable wealth and non-marketable wealth. Why did they make this distinction?

96 'An important criticism of the wealth tax proposals is that they do not distinguish the source of wealth.' What are the sources of wealth? Why do you think the critics believe that a wealth tax should distinguish between these sources?

97 In the UK all taxes combined are only slightly progressive.
a Why should this be so when it is clearly government policy to reduce inequality?
b If the tax system has relatively little effect on the distribution of income, how does the government reduce the degree of inequality?

98 'Statistics showing the *current* distribution of income can be rather misleading because the inequality of lifetime incomes is less than the inequality of income distribution observed at any particular point in time.' Explain.

99 Many of the benefits provided by the state are of the flat-rate or universal type (e.g. state pensions, child benefits, the education service, and the health service) where rich and poor are entitled to the same benefits. How can such a system be said to reduce the inequality of income?

100 a How can economic theory be used to justify an equal distribution of income?
b What are the main arguments against an equal distribution of income?

101 What are the main forms in which personal wealth is held?

102 What purposes would a wealth tax serve which are not already served by the Capital Transfer Tax (the Gift Tax)?

Data response question

103 This question is based on Figure 36.

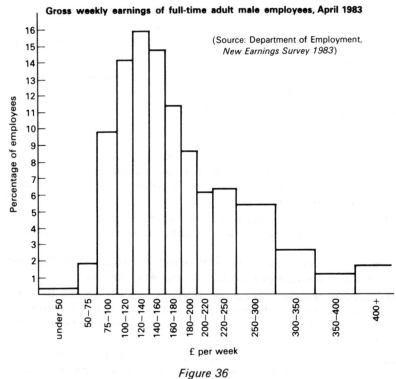

Figure 36

a Describe and explain the distribution of earnings shown in Figure 36.
b What policies might bring about a more equal distribution of earnings?

F Public ownership and control

Short answer questions

104 Most of the nationalised industries have some degree of monopoly power, but several of them, in certain markets, are also monopsonists. Can you give some examples of this latter situation?

105 'Their dependence on government as *shareholder*, *banker*, and *paymaster* permeates the entire operations of the nationalised industries.'
Explain, in the context of the quotation, the relationships in italics.

106 'Governments in the past have tried to reduce the rate of inflation by holding down the nationalised industries' prices, but the cost of such policies can become unacceptably high.'
Explain what is meant by 'the cost of such policies'.

107 Nationalised industries are subject to social and political pressures which oblige them to conduct some operations which are not commercially viable. How are the losses on these particular operations financed?

108 Why is the rate of profit (expressed as a rate of return on capital employed) an unsatisfactory indicator of efficiency in nationalised industries?

109 Give some examples of nationalised industries using their monopoly power to practice price discrimination.

110 Among the reasons advanced for the state ownership of industry is the argument that certain industries are 'natural monopolies'. Explain the meaning of this term and provide some examples.

111 It has been suggested that the efficiency of nationalised industries should not be judged solely on the basis of their ability to meet financial targets; financial information should be supplemented by the publication of *performance indicators*. Can you suggest some such indicators?

112 Indicate some of the ways in which governments might exercise a high degree of control over the operations of privately owned enterprise without resorting to complete public ownership.

Multiple choice questions

113 Which of the following is *not* true of a nationalised industry?

A It is managed by a Board appointed by the responsible Minister.
B The methods by which it raises funds for capital investment are subject to Treasury control.
C It is not allowed to charge prices which exceed average cost.
D It is expected to earn some target rate of return on its net assets.

Questions **114** and **115** are based on the following organisations, all of which form part of the government's framework for influencing the structure and performance of industry.

A EDC
B MMC
C ECGD
D FFI

114 Which of them is concerned primarily with the provision of finance for investment?

115 Which of them is one of several such bodies formed to consider the longer-term problems and prospects of individual industries?

116 If a nationalised industry makes a net profit, it may use the surplus to
1 reduce prices.
2 raise the wages of its workers.
3 finance new investment.

A 1, 2, and 3   C 2 and 3 only   E 3 only
B 1 and 2 only   D 1 only

Data response question

117 This question is based on Figure 37 which illustrates a relationship between costs and revenue similar to that which applies in a number of nationalised industries.

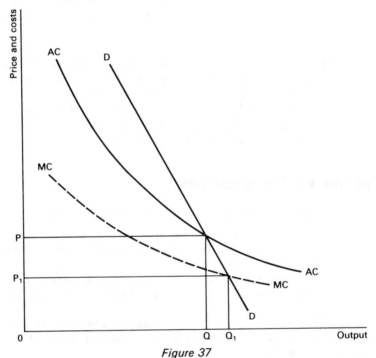

Figure 37

a (i) What conditions of production are illustrated by the cost curves in Figure 37?
(ii) In what type of industry are they likely to apply?
b Explain the problem facing a nationalised industry in the situation depicted in Figure 37, if it is obliged to obey the following guidelines.
(i) 'Nationalised industries' revenue should normally cover their accounting costs in full'.
(ii) 'In addition to covering their accounting costs, prices need to be reasonably related to costs at the margin.'

Answers

Answers to part 1

Short answer questions

1 a The economic resources or factors of production (i.e. land, labour and capital). **b** '... scarce means which have alternative uses'.

2 These goods are scarce in the sense that the supplies of them are insufficient to fully satisfy people's wants.

3 The curve shows the productive *potential* of an economy, that is, the various combinations of goods and services which could be produced if *all* the economy's resources were fully employed.

4 In economic analysis, the theory of distribution is concerned with the way in which the national income is distributed in the form of wages, interest, rent and profits.

5 a The high price of potatoes would probably cause farmers to allocate more land to potatoes in the next growing season.

b There will be some substitution of electricity for other forms of energy and an increased demand for (and supply of) electrical appliances.

c Some resources will move out of the production of tea; more resources will tend to move into the production of coffee. These movements will be responses to a fall in the price of tea and a rise in the price of coffee.

d Various forms of public entertainment (especially cinemas) will suffer a fall in demand. Revenues and profits will fall and resources will move out of these activities.

6 a A command economy. **b** A market economy. **c** A command economy. **d** A market economy.

7 a Defence, flood control installations, lighthouses, police protection.

b Non-rivalry in consumption. This means that the benefits derived by any one person from a collective good in no way diminishes the benefits available to others.

8 a By the use of such measures as indirect taxes, subsidies and price controls.

b Imports can be restricted by means of tariffs and quotas. Exports can be subsidised and exporting firms given preferential treatment in the market for loans. Devaluation may stimulate exports *and* reduce imports.

c Proposed mergers may be vetoed by the government, but public policy may also encourage integration by the provision of public funds.

d Financial inducements may be used to encourage firms to establish enterprises in high-unemployment areas. Planning controls may be used to restrict development in other areas.

9 a Social benefits in the form of increased recreational facilities – swimming, sailing and fishing. Social costs in the form of disruption and movement of families displaced by the reservoir and in the form of longer journeys between villages that were formerly a short journey from each other.
b Social benefits in the form of increased values of neighbouring properties and more pleasing aspects for passers-by.
c Significant social benefits in the form of greatly reduced atmospheric pollution.
d Social benefits in the form of a greatly improved environment (removal of unsightly pylons and poles).
e Social costs in the form of loss of income suffered by shops, garages, cafes, etc., as a result of the diversion away from the town. Social benefits in the form of reduced congestion, pollution and danger on roads within the town and in the form of speedier journeys on the by-pass.

10 a Positive **b** Normative **c** Normative **d** Normative **e** Positive.

11 It is only possible to make a limited number of observations in order to test the validity of the theory and it is always possible that, in the future, some observation will be made which refutes the theory.

12 Economic theories can only be tested over time. It is necessary to make careful observations and to record all the relevant data. This information is then subjected to statistical analysis as a means of checking whether the relationships expounded in the theory are supported by the facts.

13 C **14** C **15** D

16 C It would not be possible to confine the services to those who are prepared to pay for them.

17 D **18** B **19** E **20** A

True or false?

21 a False [Scarcity refers to the availability of goods and services relative to people's wants. Increasing money income does nothing directly to reduce this scarcity.]
b True **c** False **d** True **e** False **f** False **g** True.

Data response question

22 a The curve will appear as a line concave to the origin (similar to Figure 1) joining a point on the X-axis (120 units) to a point on the Y-axis (200 units).
b The information does not allow us to compare the labour productivity in the two industries because they are not producing the same good. For this purpose we would need to know the relative values of the two products.
c 20 units of Y.   **d** 'increases'.

Answers to part 2

Short answer questions

1 a Durable consumer good **b** Services **c** Capital **d** Services **e** Capital
f Capital.

2 The statement is true. Over the years most agricultural land has been 'improved' by drainage, irrigation, fencing, ditching, and the application of fertilisers.

3 *Replaceable:* animal and vegetable products (the products of forestry, farming, and fishing).
Non-replaceable: minerals (e.g. coal, oil, and metal ores).

4 It is the sacrifice of the consumption goods which could have been produced by the resources which have to be diverted to the production of capital goods.

5 Active population $= \left(\dfrac{65}{100} \times \dfrac{60}{100} \times 50 \text{ million} \right) + \left(\dfrac{5}{100} \times \dfrac{40}{100} \times 50 \text{ million} \right)$
$= 20.5$ million.
Weekly supply of labour $= 20.5$ million $\times 40$ hours $= 820$ million worker hours.

6 Output-per-worker-hour.

7 *Advantages* Higher productivity makes possible a higher real income and a shorter working week. Specialisation makes possible a greater use of machinery so that work will be physically less arduous.
Disadvantages: Work tends to be more monotonous and it is difficult for a worker to develop pride in his or her work. Workers have a very narrow range of skills and are more vulnerable to changes in the demands for products and to changes in the techniques of production.

8 (*f*)   **9** (*d*)   **10** (*e*)   **11** (*a*)   **12** (*b*)

13 A highly specialised factor of production (e.g. a blast furnace or an atomic physicist) is extremely efficient in the particular function for which it has been designed or trained but it is likely to be totally unsuitable for, or very inefficient in, any other use. One cost of high productivity is a serious loss in mobility.

14 a No. The profit-maximising entrepreneur would choose the least-cost combination. Since we have no information on the prices of the factors of production, the least-cost combination cannot be determined.
b We can eliminate method B because it is certain to be more costly than method D.

146

15 a OM_2 **b** OM_1 **c** OM.

16 The risks associated with the success or failure of a business enterprise are not insurable; they cannot be assessed by using the laws of probability. The risks associated with other types of labour (e.g. physical injury) are insurable.

17 a Low **b** High **c** High **d** High **e** Low **f** High.

18 Diminishing returns is associated with changes in output in the short-run. It refers to returns to the variable factor when one or more of the other factors of production is fixed in supply. Diminishing returns occurs when the marginal product of the variable factor begins to decline.

Diseconomies of scale refers to changes in output in the long-run, that is, when the amounts of all the factors can be changed. In this case the changes in output are related to the scale of production. Diseconomies of scale occur when the increases in output are less than proportionate to the increases in the scale of production.

Multiple choice questions

19 E [Investment means the creation of real capital, including additions to stock.]

20 A **21** C **22** E **23** C

24 D [MP begins to fall while AP is still rising.]

True or false?

25 a True **b** True

[When productivity is falling, total output may be increased by employing more workers.]

c False **d** False **e** True **f** False

[The latter part of the statement refers to *increasing* returns.]

g True

[When one factor is variable and other factors are fixed, the proportions between them are variable.]

h True.

Data response questions

26 (i) (c) (ii) (b) (iii) (a)

Increases in the stock of, and improvements in the quality of, capital lead to great increases in the productivity of labour in the extractive industries. This releases manpower for work in manufacturing and construction. Similar developments lead to rising productivity in manufacturing. The resultant rises in productivity and changes in the methods of production lead to demands for a wide variety of services.

Some of these services are associated with increasing demands for leisure activities (e.g. entertainment, private motoring, tourism, meals consumed outside the home, etc.). As incomes rise, more and more public services (e.g. health and education) are demanded and the increasing complexity of life and work brings increasing demands for such services as law, accountancy, insurance, banking, and so on. Increases in the scale of production tend to increase the proportion of management and administrative personnel.

27 a (i) Table A because one of the factors of production is fixed. (ii) Table B because all the factors are variable.

b Table A because the marginal product of the variable factor is declining as total output increases.

c Table B because total output increases *more than proportionately* as the scale of production increases.

d The conventional two-dimensional graph can only be used to show the related movements of two variables. Table B illustrates the relationships between three variables.

Answers to part 3

Short answer questions

1 **a**, **b**, **e**.

2 **a** £7.33 [Total variable cost = £22, average variable cost = £22 ÷ 3.]
 b Decreasing returns (marginal cost is increasing).

3 **a** Total variable cost **b** Total costs **c** Average variable cost **d** Average fixed cost **e** Average total cost.

4 '... *increases* at a *diminishing* rate ...'

5 It would need to produce a minimum hourly output of 1200 units and hence would require 12 of A; 6 of B; 5 of C; and 4 of D.

6 Bulk buying of raw materials common to both products (e.g. sugar). Lower average distribution costs since many market outlets sell both products.
Financial economies – larger firms generally obtain loans at lower interest rates.
Administrative economies (centralisation of administrative functions).
Risk-bearing economies (diversification of output).

7 Diseconomies of scale (total output has increased less-than-proportionately).

8 An *enterprise* is a unit of ownership (generally described as a firm).
An *establishment* is a unit of production (e.g. farm, factory, mine).

9 Demand for variety of product (e.g. three-wheelers).
Markets for some cars limited by income (e.g. luxury limousines, expensive sports cars).

10 Measures which use total employment as the indicator of size understate the importance of firms in capital intensive industries (e.g. oil, chemicals) where the value of output and the value of assets employed may be much greater than in firms in other industries which are employing more workers.
  The value of sales may also be misleading in the sense that firms producing very expensive products by capital-intensive methods may be relatively small in terms of the amount of labour employed. There is also a problem of aggregation. The five largest firms may comprise a group of firms of approximately equal size, or it may be a group made up, say, of two extremely large firms and three relatively small firms.

11 Ownership lies in the hands of the shareholders while, in the larger firm, control is exercised by a board of directors or salaried managers whose personal stake in the ownership of the firm may be relatively small.

12 The word 'public' is used to distinguish this type of company from the private company. A public company may offer its shares to the general public; a private company may not do so. The word 'limited' indicates that the shareholders' liabilities for the debts of the company are limited to the value of the shares they have agreed to buy.

13 *Advantage:* Interest on loan capital is regarded as a cost of production and qualifies for tax relief in assessing the liability for corporation tax.
Disadvantage: Interest charges must be met each year regardless of the company's financial performance and profitability.

14 '... degree of *liquidity* for what would otherwise be an *illiquid* asset.'

15 a 3:1.
b Debenture-holders' loans are secured by some charge on the company's assets. In the event of default, these assets may be seized and realised by the debenture-holders.
c $7\frac{1}{2}$ per cent.

16 To remove large discrepancies in regional unemployment rates.
To increase economic stability by encouraging economic diversification of industrial structure in different regions.
To reduce problems of congestion in the great conurbations.
To ensure that social costs and benefits are taken into account when location decisions are made.

17 a When the industry 'breaks up' into a large number of specialist suppliers of components, the small firm is able to achieve significant economies of scale by concentrating on one small piece of the final product.
b Small firms can join together to operate (i) joint research establishments, (ii) cooperative bulk-buying agencies, and (iii) large units of capital on the basis of joint ownership and shared usage.
c When a variety of designs and models is demanded, small firms will predominate because the economies of mass production depend upon a large market for a standardised product.

18 The National Coal Board may be faced with the problem of operating high-cost pits in areas with few or no alternative means of employment. Closing these pits would reduce the average cost of coal but create serious social problems in the form of heavy local unemployment.
British Rail may be operating loss-making lines to remote areas with relatively small populations. Closing such lines would improve profitability but may create serious social (and economic) problems where such areas are heavily dependent on the railway network.

19 a The *dividend* is the value of the distributed profits expressed as a percentage of the value of the share capital.

b The *yield* is the value of the distributed profits expressed as a percentage of the market value of the shares.

20 *Rationalisation* describes the restructuring of a firm or industry. It may take the form of more standardisation (reducing the range of products), greater specialisation, the closure of less efficient plants, the integration of plants to achieve greater economies of scale, and so on.

Multiple choice questions

21 C **22** C **23** E **24** B **25** D **26** A **27** B [the National Coal Board] **28** D **29** C.

True or false?

30 a False **b** True
c True   [If there were no Stock Exchange, or something similar, long-term securities would be very illiquid assets.]
d True **e** False
f False   [Vertical integration does not necessarily lead to increased market shares at the different stages of production.]
g False **h** False **i** True **j** False

Data response questions

31 a A trust is a legal device by which property may be vested in nominal owners (the trustees) to be used by them for the benefit of others. A unit trust is a method of pooling the resources of small investors so that their combined contributions can be invested in a wide range of securities. The money is invested by professional managers. The investors in a unit trust purchase *units* in the trust fund, the market value of which varies according to the profitability of the companies in which the funds are invested. Units can be resold to the fund at any time at prices which are announced in the national press.
b An increase in the market value of the units.
c The income on preference shares is in the form of fixed interest (unless they are participating preference shares) and a rise in the general level of profits will not normally increase their market prices.
d When market rates of interest are falling.
e Gross yield is the money value of the dividend expressed as a percentage of the market value of the unit. 'Gross' indicates that no allowance has been made for income tax deductions.

(a)

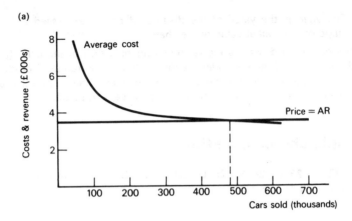

(b)

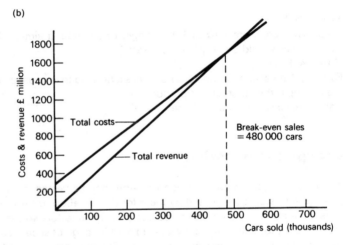

Figure 38

32 a See Figure 38 (a). **b** See Figure 38 (b). **c** 480 000 cars.
d A restriction on home sales leads to a fall in output and an increase in average cost (AC). This increase in AC could lead to an increase in prices and hence to a serious loss of sales in the very competitive export markets.

33 a Ownership of the source of aggregates provides security of supplies. It also reduces transport costs because the producers of concrete can process the aggregates into a concrete mixture on the site of a quarry.
b *Vertical integration forwards:* suppliers of aggregates merge with suppliers of concrete.
Vertical integration backwards: suppliers of concrete take over a firm producing aggregates.

Independent suppliers of aggregates would lose their market outlets if several makers of ready-mixed concrete took over quarries to supply themselves with the required aggregates.

c Companies which are vertically integrated backwards into raw material suppliers may refuse to supply companies who will be competing with them in the market for the final product. Alternatively they may supply the raw materials to these competitors but at relatively high prices.

Answers to part 4

Short answer questions

1 a (i) **b** (ii) and (iii).

2 a The dependency ratio. **b** The infant mortality rate.

3 a 'geometric'. **b** Disease, epidemics, plagues, wars, and famine.

4 The significant increase in the number of married women entering the labour force.

5 a 10 120 000 **b** 4 958 800.

6 The economist is interested in those things which determine people's economic welfare and for this purpose it is the relationship between the number of people and the supply of economic resources which is relevant, rather than the ratio of people to land area. Hence it is the supplies of fertile land and mineral resources, the supply (and quality) of capital, the climate, and the skills of the people which must be related to the size of the poulation when deciding whether a country is under- or over-populated.

7 There would be an increase in expenditure on various health services since the need for health care increases sharply in the older age groups. The proportion of social expenditure devoted to state pensions would also tend to increase. The effect on the dependency ratio would depend on the extent to which the increases in the numbers and proportion of elderly people in the population are offset by a fall in the birth rate. It is possible that a fall in social spending on young people might offset increased social spending on the elderly.

8 Assume the total population = 100. Then the farming population = 70, the non-farming population = 30, and the annual increase in population = 1.5. If the whole of this increase is to be absorbed by the non-farm sector, this sector of the population must increase from 30 to 31.5, that is, by 5 per cent per annum. Hence in order to *reduce* the rural surplus of labour, non-agricultural employment must increase by more than 5 per cent per annum.

Multiple choice questions

9 B

10 C   [The official dependency ratio is a relationship between the numbers in different age groups. It is not affected by the activity rate in a particular age group.]

11 D   **12** D   **13** B

14 a True   [These children are part of the existing population.]
b True   **c** True   **d** False   **e** True
f True   [The fall in the birth rate may be due to a fall in the numbers of women in the child-bearing age groups; the fertility rate may be unchanged.]

Data response question

15 Country A

a A high birth rate and a high death rate.

b A relatively low life expectancy.

c A low proportion of the population in the working age groups.

d A high dependency ratio due to the large proportion of the population under fifteen.

e The 'fir tree' shape of the age distribution is due to a high birth rate and a high death rate. These are indicators of a low level of economic development.

Country B

A low birth rate and a low death rate.

A relatively high life expectancy.

A high proportion of the population in the working age groups.

A relatively high dependency ratio due to the large proportion of elderly people.

The 'beehive' shape of the age distribution is due to a low birth rate and low death rate. These features are typical of a developed economy.

Answers to part 5

1 Prices

Short answer questions

1 Advertisements in local newspapers; window advertising; 'for sale' boards; and for cars, displays on garage forecourts.

2 Since all economic goods and services have money prices we are able to compare the value of one commodity in terms of another. In other words, price tells us what one thing is worth in terms of another. Thus, the wage rate enables a worker to measure the exchange value of one hour's work in terms of a wide variety of goods and services.

3 A demand curve indicates the amounts which consumers *are prepared* to buy at different prices. The supply curve tells us the amounts which suppliers are prepared to supply at different prices. Only at one price will these two quantities be equated and this price determines the *realised* demand (and realised supply).

4 (*a*) The price of commodity *X*, (*b*) the relevant time period.

5 Changes in (*a*) consumers' real income, (*b*) consumers' tastes, (*c*) the prices of complements and substitutes, (*d*) taxation, (*e*) population, (*f*) advertising.

6 a (i) and (iv) **b** (ii) and (iii).

7 (*b*) and (*c*).

8 a Good X and good Y are complements (i.e. jointly demanded).
b Good Z and good Y are substitutes (i.e. in competitive demand).

9 Total revenue will increase by 10 per cent.

10 A consumer aims to maximise the satisfaction obtained from some given amount of income. Thus, she must take into account (*a*) the marginal utilities of the commodities purchased, *and* (*b*) their market prices. If the last pound spent on good X yields more utility than the last pound spent on good Y, the total utility could be increased by switching some spending from Y to X.

11 The demand curve for good A is of the normal shape since an increase in price leads to a fall in the quantity demanded. It is, however, an inferior good since the demand falls when income increases.

12 a 0P   **b** Q_1Q_2 **c** (i) P_1P_2 (ii) $P_1P_2 \times 0Q_2$

13 The quantity demanded will increase by 15 per cent.

14 a The commodities are in joint supply.
   b The commodities are in competitive demand (i.e. substitute goods).
   c The commodities are in joint demand (i.e. complementary goods).

15 a 1.6   **b** 0.8   **c** 9p   **d** (i) 8p (ii) 140 units.

16 See Figure 39.

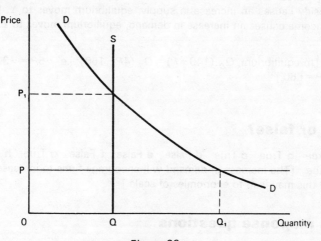

Figure 39

S represents the fixed supply of tickets. 0P is the fixed price, which is well below the free market price ($0P_1$). QQ_1 is the unsatisfied demand at the fixed price.

17 Shortages created by prices being held (usually by law) at levels well below the free market prices.

18 We use the formula,

$$\frac{\text{proportion of tax borne by producer}}{\text{proportion of tax borne by consumer}} = \frac{\text{elasticity of demand}}{\text{elasticity of supply}}$$

$$= \frac{1.5}{0.5}$$

$$= \frac{3}{1}$$

Hence, producer pays $\frac{3}{4}$ of tax = 3p
consumer pays $\frac{1}{4}$ of tax = 1p

19 a $0P_1$ **b** Quantity consumed increases from 0Q to $0Q_1$, and price falls from 0P to $0P_1$.   **c** $GF \times 0Q_1$ **d** $GQ_1 \times 0Q_1$ (for each unit sold producers receive FQ_1 from consumers and GF in the form of a subsidy).

157

Multiple choice questions

20 C **21** D [See note on elasticity at the end of Chapter 14 in *Introductory Economics.*]

22 C [C represents a change in price; the other options refer to changes in the conditions of demand.]

23 E **24** A **25** C **26** C **27** A **28** D **29** B **30** C

31 E [Indirect tax caused a reduction in supply, equilibrium moved to S. Subsidy causes an increase in supply, equilibrium moves to Y. Increase in income causes an increase in demand, equilibrium moves to Z.]

32 C

33 B [In equilibrium, Q_d $(140 - P) = Q_s$ $(4P - 160)$; i.e. $-5P = -300$ $\therefore P = £60.$]

34 C

True or false?

35 **a** True **b** True **c** True **d** False **e** False **f** False **g** True **h** True **i** True [The increase in demand will encourage firms to increase output and this may lead to economies of scale.]

Data response questions

36 a See Figure 40.

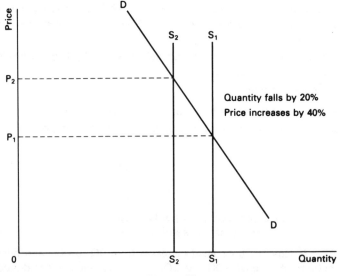

Quantity falls by 20%
Price increases by 40%

Figure 40

Figure 40 shows how shifts in short-run supply curves for agricultural products combined with a relatively inelastic demand curve have relatively large effects on price. These movements in supply will be unplanned if they are due to variations in weather conditions from one growing season to another.

b It means that stocks of potatoes cannot be held to smooth out the shifts in supply due to annual variations in output.

c The quantity of potatoes available to consumers fell by 20 per cent. As a result, prices rose by 40 per cent.

$$\text{Elasticity of demand} = \frac{20\%}{40\%} = 0.5$$

d Since demand is inelastic, the increase in price would lead to an increase in total revenue and the incomes of potato producers would increase.

37 a They will be very inelastic.

b If new investment in the mining of ores has not been taking place for several years, the capacity of the industry will not have increased and, perhaps, the replacement of older equipment may have been neglected. This lack of investment will restrict the ability to produce and, in the short run, supply will be very inelastic. An increase in demand, therefore, will lead to a sharp increase in the price of metals and hence raise costs in the engineering industries.

c Mining industries make use of heavy and expensive capital equipment so that a high proportion of total costs consists of fixed costs (capital costs). Reducing output will reduce variable costs (marginal costs), but, because these costs are a relatively small proportion of total costs, the effect of cutting back production will be that the proportionate fall in output will be much greater than the proportionate fall in total costs. In the short run, therefore, the response to a fall in demand is not likely to be a reduction in output.

2 Markets

Short answer questions

38 *Market* demand curves will be of the normal shape. Under conditions of perfect competition, the individual firm 'sees' the demand curve for its product as being perfectly elastic because variations in *its own* output have no influence on price.

39 Economic theory assumes that a firm's short-run MC and AC curves are U-shaped. There will be some point, therefore, where, at the ruling price, the rising MC curve cuts the price line and total profits will begin to fall.

40 It is that rate of profit which is just sufficient to persuade a firm to stay in its existing line of business.

41 **a** $0Q_2$ **b** $0Q_3$
c The firm is in short-run equilibrium because it is making abnormal profits. In the long-run, these profits will persuade other firms to enter the industry, total supply will increase and market price will fall until all firms are earning normal profits.

42 **a** When output is zero there will be no receipts, but fixed costs must still be met.
b Since the total revenue curve is a straight line, price must be constant. The gradient of this line is equal to total revenue divided by total output, that is, average revenue or price.
c (ii)   **d** They are equal.

43 (c) leave output unchanged. The firm is in equilibrium, producing at the point where price = MC, and price > AC.

44 A few large suppliers; products are branded; large-scale advertising; formidable technical and financial barriers to entry.

45 Accept (a) because total revenue > total variable costs (profitable in short-run). Accept (b) because total revenue > total costs (profitable in long-run). Reject (c) because total revenue < total variable cost (unprofitable in short-run).

46 This is particularly true where the market is dominated by a few very large firms supplying goods with well-established brand names supported by heavy and continuous advertising. In order to break into this type of market a firm would have to undertake intensive market research in an attempt to estimate the likely success of a new product, and the launch of any such product would have to be accompanied by extensive advertising over a fairly long period of time.

47 **a** (ii)   **b** (iii)   **c** (i).

48 The profit-maximising monopolist equates MC and MR and since MC must be positive, then, at the equilibrium output, MR must also be positive. When MR is positive, demand is elastic.

49 Profits are maximised when MR = MC. Since in this case MC is zero, then MR must also be zero. MR is zero when elasticity of demand is unity and TR is at a maximum. Alternatively, since costs are zero, profits are maximised when TR is at a maximum and this occurs when MR is zero.

50 **a** Price £4.50; output 8 units **b** Price £3.50 **c** £3 **d** Price £3.50; output 12 units.

51 It may not be the case because the monopolist is likely to carry out organisational and structural changes which enable him to obtain economies of scale. These economies would mean that the monopolist's cost curves would be lower than those of a competitive industry. It is *possible*, therefore, that output may be higher and price may be lower than those obtained in the competitive industry.

52 a A discriminating monopoly has the ability to sell identical products in different markets at different prices.
b (i) Time is used to separate markets in
rail transport – low off-peak fares.
electricity supply – reduced prices for off-peak electricity.
telephone services – lower charges in off-peak periods.
(ii) Age is used to separate markets in
public transport – lower fares for school children and pensioners.
some forms of entertainment – lower prices for children and pensioners.

53 a All costs are fixed costs. Maximum profits are achieved by charging a price of £4. (TR = £320; TC = 240; profits = £80.)
b £4
c £3

54 (*a*) and (*d*)   [(*b*) and (*c*) are examples of oligopolies.]

55 Any change in price by an oligopolist is certain to affect rival firms. There will be great uncertainty as to the nature and scale of reaction by these competing firms. For example, a cut in price by one firm might provoke a lowering of price by the other firms. The result could be that no firm increases its share of the market but they all suffer a fall in total revenue.

Common forms of non-price competition are advertising, trading stamps, free gifts, after-sales service, free delivery, free samples, part-exchanges, etc.

56 An extremely successful and sustained advertising campaign could lead to a substantial increase in the size of the market. The resulting increase in output might enable the firm to achieve economies of scale such that average total cost (including advertising costs) was less than it was before the advertising campaign was undertaken.

Multiple choice questions

57 B   [The individual firm does not *aim* to produce where AC is at a minimum; it is forced into this position by competition from other firms.]
58 D   **59** A   **60** C   **61** E   **62** C   **63** A   **64** B   **65** E   **66** A   **67** D   **68** D
69 B   **70** E   **71** A.

True or false?

72 a True [Output is determined by MR and MC; a change in fixed costs does not affect MC.]

b False

c False [Monopoly refers to a situation where there is a single *supplier*. Several firms may collaborate to market their outputs as a single seller.]

d False [The *market* price is not fixed; it is determined by the market demand and supply curves.]

e True **f** False **g** True

h True [Advertising aims to create brand loyalties and hence diminish the attractiveness of substitutes.]

Data response questions

73 a A mature market exists when most of the potential consumers already possess one or more of the consumer durables supplied by the industry. It is, therefore, highly dependent on replacement rather than new demand.

b Many electrical appliances such as cookers, washing machines, vacuum cleaners; television sets; clothing and footwear; household crockery and cutlery, etc.

c A reduction in the range of products which makes possible a greater utilisation of standardised components.

d If, in a particular market for cars, the demand is largely a replacement demand, then any growth in the total market is largely dependent upon the possibilities of increasing the number of 'two-car' (or 'three-car') families. If it is true that the marginal utility of an extra vehicle diminishes rapidly, then it would seem that only a fall in the price of cars (relative to other prices) could bring about any significant expansion of the total market.

e The growing significance of replacement demand has obliged producers of motor cars to encourage an increased frequency of replacement by using technical innovations to produce a steady stream of improvements in styling and performance.

74 a Imperfect competition – demand curve is downward-sloping.

b 9000 units.

c (i) Yes, because total profits will increase.

(ii) Under existing market conditions, maximum profit of £41 000 is achieved when output is 9000 units.

Profit on new contract = TR – TC
$$= £75\,000 - £57\,000$$
$$= £18\,000$$

To calculate profit on additional sales it is necessary to bear in mind the fact that total costs of £57 000 will be incurred in meeting the new contract. Thus, the first 4000 units supplied to the market will incur total costs of £85 000 − £57 000 = £28 000. The total costs of supplying 5000 units to the market will be £91 000 − £57 000 = £34 000, and so on.

The details of the total revenues obtained from market sales will remain as in the original table. The situation regarding costs and revenues in respect of market sales (after the acceptance of the contract) will be as follows

Output (000s)	Total costs (£000s)	Total revenue (£000s)	Profit (£000s)
4	28	76	48
5	34	90	56
6	42	102	60
7	53	112	59

Maximum profit on additional output = £60 000
Hence total maximum profit if new contract is accepted

$$= £60 000 + £18 000$$
$$= £78 000$$

75 Points which might be made are

(*a*) Industry is capital-intensive and technical progress is rapid − hence large funds will be needed to cover depreciation and frequent modernisation programmes. This might justify a high rate of profit if a substantial part of total profits is being ploughed back.

(*b*) A high rate of profit might also be justified if there is heavy expenditure on research and development.

(*c*) Given the UK's relatively poor performance in export markets over recent years, there would be some reluctance to recommend changes which might prejudice this firm's good record in overseas markets.

(*d*) On the other hand, if this firm is efficient, why does it need the protection of a tariff? The firm might argue that a secure home market enables it to achieve economies of scale which help it to compete in overseas markets. Against this, however, the interests of home consumers must also be given due consideration.

Answers to part 6

1 The national income

Short answer questions

1 National income = GNP at factor cost − capital consumption.

2 This would lead to multiple counting because the inputs of some industries are the outputs of other industries. For example, to add the value of the output of millers to the value of the output of bakers would involve counting the flour content of bread, cakes, etc., twice.

3 This income accrues in foreign currencies and represents a claim on the outputs of other countries and hence adds to the UK national income.

4 Only that part of the sale price of the car which represents factor income for services rendered in supplying the car would be counted in the national income. The difference between the *trader's* purchase price and the sale price is assumed to represent payments for services rendered plus profit.

5 We must deduct all transfer payments (e.g. pensions and other social security benefits) and add all factor income which has not accrued to households (e.g. retained profits).

6 What is produced must either be sold or added to stocks. In order to make expenditure = output, it is necessary to define expenditure so as to include the actual market transactions *and* the additions to stocks.

7 This is a common mistake. Where the money originates is not relevant here. What does matter is whether the payment is made for the services of a factor of production; whether, in fact, there has been a corresponding contribution to national output. The policemen's services do represent a contribution to national output.

8 (*a*), (*c*), (*e*), and (*f*).

9 a The services of housewives are clearly a major contribution to real national income. They are not included in the official statistics because no reasonably accurate estimate can be made of their value.
b No. National income statistics are mainly used for comparisons over time. The omission does not invalidate their use for this purpose providing there is no serious change in the proportion of real national income

accounted for by housewives' services. It does not invalidate comparisons with other countries if they use similar statistical conventions.

10 The item 'income from self-employment' is clearly made up of wages, interest, rent, and profits. If we assume that half of this item comprises wages, the total return to labour will be equal to, income from employment $+\frac{1}{2}$ income from self-employment. This total amounts to about 75 per cent of Gross National Product.

11 We can use the price index to measure changes in national income at constant prices. The national income in year 5 expressed in terms of the prices ruling in year 1 is equal to

$$\frac{£20\,000 \text{ million}}{1} \times \frac{100}{140} = £14\,285.7 \text{ million (approx.)}$$

Thus, in real terms, the national income increased by 42.85 per cent.

12 **a** GDP at market prices = £76 million.
b GNP at market prices = £77 million.
c National income = £60 million.

13 The movements in the figures for national income would provide no information on such matters as changes in (*a*) the distribution of income, (*b*) population, (*c*) the composition of total output, (*d*) environmental conditions (e.g. social costs and benefits), (*e*) civil liberties, (*f*) the amount of leisure time available, and so on.

14 The rate of exchange may not be a good indicator of the relative domestic purchasing powers of different currencies. Only the prices of goods and services which are traded internationally are likely to affect the exchange rate which may also be significantly affected by capital movements and speculative activities.

Multiple choice questions

15 C [Investment grants are transfer payments.]
16 B **17** C
18 C [*Loss* of factor income = £10 000 + £8000 = £18 000. *Increase* in factor income = £6000 + £2000 = £8000. Change in factor income = −£10 000.]
19 D **20** D **21** A **22** C.

True or false?

23 **a** False [Most local authority expenditure consists of payments for goods and services.]
b True
c False [Estimates are made of some outputs, (e.g. the value of services rendered by owner-occupied houses).]
d True **e** False **f** False [These payments are regarded as a return to labour.]

Data response questions

24 a Note: gross profits are disposed of in three ways – one part is distributed as dividends (this appears in households' income), one part is retained and one part is taken in taxation.

Income account	**£ million**
Households' income from sale of factor services	20 000
Retained profits	1 000
Profits taken in taxes	1 500
GNP at factor cost	22 500

Expenditure account	
Consumption spending by households	16 000
Government spending on goods and services	4 000
Gross investment	4 000
Exports	4 000
Less imports	– 4 500
GNP at market prices	23 500
Less indirect taxes	– 1 000
GNP at factor cost	22 500

b This presentation is based on the principles of double-entry book-keeping and clearly shows that there are two aspects to every transaction.

By presenting the separate accounts for each broad sector we are able to see more clearly the flows of income and expenditure between them (i.e. how the expenditure of one sector becomes the income of another sector). This is a useful exercise because later work on the determination of national income requires us to understand the nature of the relationships between the different sectors of the economy; normally flow charts are used to explain these relationships.

25 a 100; 150; 150; 400

b 400

c Value added by Firm 1 = 100
Value added by Firm 2 = 150
Value added by Firm 3 = 150

Sum of values added = 400

Value of final products = 400 = sales to households

2 Wages

26 a It would move upwards. **b** It would move downwards.

27 a $0W \times 0Q$ **b** $AQ \times 0Q$.
c That part of the MRP curve which lies below the ARP curve.
d It is perfectly elastic.

28 a 4 **b** None, because £145 exceeds the ARP of labour at all levels of employment.

29 a (ii) and (iv) **b** (i).

30 No. If all occupations paid the same wage rate, supply would exceed demand for the more congenial jobs and the opposite would apply for the less attractive jobs. Wage differentials would develop in order to eliminate these surpluses and shortages.

31 The purchasing power of the weekly wage in year 4 expressed in terms of year 1 prices is

$$\frac{£180}{1} \times \frac{120}{150} = £144$$

Real wages have increased by 44 per cent.

32 (*a*) Differences in pension rights (e.g. contributory and non-contributory schemes).
(*b*) Different holiday entitlements.
(*c*) A wide range of other fringe benefits such as subsidised meals, subsidised travelling expenses, subsidised housing, company cars, etc.

33 The increase in the weekly wage rate increases labour costs per unit of output in the ratio $\frac{112.5}{100}$.
The reduction in the working week increases labour costs per unit of output in the ratio $\frac{42}{40}$.
The increase in productivity reduces labour costs per unit of output in the ratio $\frac{100}{110}$.
The net change on the base of $100 = \frac{100}{1} \times \frac{112.5}{100} \times \frac{42}{40} \times \frac{100}{110} = 107.386$.
Labour costs per unit of output increase by 7.4 per cent (approx.).

34 Since the worker chooses to work 38 hours per week when the wage rate is £5 per hour, the income effect has predominated.

35 Although the individual worker may supply fewer labour hours when the wage rate exceeds a certain level, an industry can increase its labour supply by recruiting more workers at higher wage levels.

36 a (i) **b** (ii) and (iii).

37 (*a*) Surgeon: high level of ability and long training period, qualification by examination. (*c*) Underwriters: restricted entry and substantial financial resources required. (*d*) Architect: lengthy training period, entry restricted by examination requirements.

Multiple choice questions

38 D **39** C
40 B [The increased availability of cheaper building land will increase the demand for houses and factories so that the demand for building workers will increase. The demand curve for this type of labour will move to the right. The other changes would not move the demand curve.]
41 C

True or false?

42 a False **b** True
   c True [The *percentage* wage differentials would be reduced.]
   d False
   e False [Real wages have tended to move very much in line with productivity.]

Data response questions

43 (*a*) The allocation of (i) the maximum points for each feature, and (ii) the points for the particular feature in any job, may still give rise to dispute because there is a subjective element in the judgement.
   (*b*) There is also the major problem of moving from 'points to pence'. How are we to decide the money values of the points differences?
   (*c*) Job evaluation must be a continuous process since the nature and content of different jobs are always changing.
   (*d*) Some account must be taken of the forces of supply and demand. The 'scientifically' established rate for the job may be too low to attract the required number of workers. If it is raised so as to increase the supply of labour, the carefully worked out structure of differentials will be seriously upset.
   (*e*) Job-evaluation techniques cannot ignore market forces but they are probably useful in removing anomalies within a wage structure determined largely by the forces of the market, custom, opinion, and various pressure groups.

44 a The difference between the movements in earnings and the movements in wage rates is explained mainly by bonus payments and payments for overtime.

b The explanation lies in the fact that the average number of hours worked increased with less short-time working and more overtime.

c The increase in earnings in manufacturing raised labour costs in the ratio $\dfrac{112.9}{100}$.

The increase in productivity reduced labour costs in the ratio $\dfrac{100}{108.3}$.

Taking labour costs from a base of 100, the net effect of these changes was $\dfrac{112.9}{100} \times \dfrac{100}{108.3} \times \dfrac{100}{1} = 104.24$.

Labour costs per unit of output rose by 4.2 per cent.

d (i) Nominal earnings rose by 12.9 per cent, prices rose by 10.7 per cent.

Change in real earnings from base of 100 $= \dfrac{112.9}{110.7} \times \dfrac{100}{1} = 101.987$

Real earnings rose by 2 per cent (approx.).

(ii) Nominal wage rate increased by 7 per cent, prices rose by 10.7 per cent.

Change in real wage rate from base of 100 $= \dfrac{107}{110.7} \times \dfrac{100}{1} = 96.66$.

The real wage rate fell by 3.3 per cent (approx.).

3 Interest

Short answer questions

45 In persuading people to lend, we are asking them to forego some current satisfactions. Since most people prefer current consumption to the promise of the same level of consumption in the future, it is necessary to offer a reward in the form of interest in order to overcome this preference for satisfactions *now*.

46 a The expected profitability is expressed as a percentage return on the money value of the capital. This return can then be compared with the cost of borrowed funds (the rate of interest). It also allows comparisons to be made with the returns on capital in other industries.

b The curve is drawn on the assumptions that other things remain equal. Hence, capital, like other factors of production will be subject to the law of diminishing returns.

c Because the calculation of *expected* profitability can be little more than intelligent guesswork.
d When the rate of interest rises, some projects which appeared profitable at the lower rate will now appear to be unprofitable and will not be undertaken.

47 a The whole curve would move to the right.
b The whole curve would move to the left.
c The whole curve would move to the left.

48 The level of real income; the social attitudes towards thrift; the availability of convenient and secure outlets for savings; the extent of contractual savings (e.g. pension funds and insurance); expectations regarding future income.

49 Much saving is contractual and habitual and is not likely to be influenced by changes in the rate of interest. The main purpose of company saving is not to achieve income in the form of interest but to provide funds for expansion and as a cushion against trade fluctuations. Similarly the motive for government saving is not the acquisition of income but the management of total demand.

50 The current rate of interest.

51 Active balances are those held for transactions and precautionary purposes. Idle balances are held for speculative purposes.

52 a The expectation of a fall in the prices of securities (i.e. a rise in the rate of interest).
b They would attempt to sell securities in order to increase their money balances.
c The increase in the market supply of securities would lower their prices and raise the rate of interest.

53 Let the market value of one of these bonds after the change in the rate of interest equal £x. Then

$$\frac{£5}{£x} \times \frac{100}{1} = 6.25$$
$$£500 = 6.25 \times £x$$
$$£x = £80$$

The market value of the securities = £80 000.

54 $\dfrac{£2.5}{£40} \times \dfrac{100}{1} = 6.25$ per cent.

55 The increased supply of securities would lower their prices and increase the rate of interest.

56 a There is some positive minimum rate of interest which is required to persuade people to surrender the advantages of holding money as an asset.
b When the rate of interest is high, security prices will be low and speculators will anticipate that the next movement in security prices will

be upwards. In anticipation of capital gains, therefore, they will be demanding securities rather than money. Also when the rate of interest is high, the opportunity cost of holding money is high.
c A reduction in the supply of money leaves people with diminished money balances; they will try to restore these balances by selling securities. In doing so they will drive down security prices and raise the rate of interest.

57 The transactions demand for money would increase and the liquidity preference curve would move to the right.

58 £6000 million.

Multiple choice questions

59 D **60** C

61 D [Whereas option D will influence the supply of money the other options will influence the demand for money (liquidity preference).]

62 C **63** D.

True or false?

64 a False **b** True **c** True **d** False **e** True.
f True [The real rate of interest will be negative when the rate of inflation exceeds the nominal rate of interest.]
g False [The firms must bear the opportunity cost (i.e. the interest foregone).]
h True

Data response questions

65 Building societies can only lend to the extent that they can borrow. The uneven flow of funds into the societies (because of changing interest rate differentials) means that in some years they have plenty of funds to lend while in other years they are short of funds. They do not ration loans by price so that in times of shortage they make borrowing conditions more restrictive (by lending a smaller proportion of the value of the house, or restricting the loans to certain types of property, or giving preference to first-time buyers).

Since the supply of houses is fixed in the short run, variations in demand (due to variations in the availability of mortgages) can have a substantial effect on house prices. Building societies supply 80 per cent of the finance for house purchase, so that house prices are largely determined by the availability of mortgage finance.

Price changes are slow to affect supply. As prices go up, new house building starts to increase, but completions lag by between 12 and 18 months. It is possible, therefore, that this time lag could increase the fluctuations in house prices. A reduction in the number of new houses *started* during a mortgage famine could lead to a reduced supply of new houses some 18 months later when there might be a mortgage glut.

One solution might be a more even rate of lending – accumulating funds for future use when funds are flowing strongly into the societies. Another might be to introduce a greater flexibility of interest charges on mortgages or to make the term of the loans variable to a greater extent.

66

	Pay-back period	
	(i) 5 years	**(ii) 20 years**
a		
Interest charges		
(at 10 per cent)	£10 000 p.a.	£10 000 p.a.
Depreciation	£20 000 p.a.	£ 5 000 p.a.
Total capital charges	£30 000 p.a.	£15 000 p.a.
b		
Interest charges		
(at 12 per cent)	£12 000 p.a.	£12 000 p.a.
Depreciation	£20 000 p.a.	£ 5 000 p.a.
Total capital charges	£32 000 p.a.	£17 000 p.a.
Absolute changes in annual capital charges	£ 2000 p.a.	£ 2000 p.a.
Percentage change in annual capital charges	6.66%	13.33%

The important point is that interest payments make up a much smaller *proportion* of capital charges in the shorter-term investment. The increase in the rate of interest from 10 per cent to 12 per cent increases the annual capital charges by 6.66 per cent for the shorter pay-back period but by 13.33 per cent for the longer period.

A great deal of manufacturing investment has a fairly short pay-back period and is therefore not likely to be much affected by changes in the rate of interest.

In general, the shorter the pay-back period for investment, the less sensitive it is likely to be to changes in the rate of interest.

4 Rent and profit

Rent

Short answer questions

67 The supply price of a factor is that price which must be paid in order to acquire its services. The opportunity cost of employing a factor is what that factor could produce (or earn) in its next most well-paid employment. Clearly the two terms are merely different ways of expressing the same idea.

68 He saw the supply of land as fixed, that is, it has no supply price. Hence he reasoned as follows. The demand for land is derived from the demand for the product of land. If the demand for corn is high, the price of corn will be high and landlords will be able to charge high rents. Thus, the price of corn determines the price of land.

69 £30

70 It can, in *monetary* terms. A person may like a job so much that he (or she) is prepared to accept lower wages for it than he (or she) might earn in a less attractive job.

71 No. Most land has alternative uses. In any one use the rent element is the excess of its current earnings over the minimum reward required to keep it in its current use.

72 It is surplus over and above the reward necessary to keep the firm in its present line of business.

73 a £8000

   b (i) No. It is still more profitable to allow development to take place than to use the land in agriculture.

   (ii) No. The tax has no effect on the demand and it cannot affect the supply of the land (assuming the owners wish to obtain some income from it).

74 a Since supply is perfectly elastic, there is no element of economic rent in the factor income.

   b SPE **c** OPES.

Multiple choice questions

75 C [What a factor might earn in its next best-paid employment does not necessarily bear any relationship to its cost of production.]

76 D

77 B

True or false

78 a True **b** True
c False [If the tax does not exceed the element of economic rent, the factor's net income will still exceed what it could earn elsewhere.]
d False [Normal profits represent transfer earnings and are not a form of economic rent.]

Profit

Short answer questions

79 a Since firms attempt to maximise profits, resources will move to those industries which are increasingly profitable and away from those industries which are making losses.
b (i) A source of funds for investment.
(ii) An incentive for entrepreneurs to take risks.
(iii) An incentive to improve efficiency – lower costs can improve profitability.

80 An economist would not agree with Mr Jones because his calculation of profit takes no account of the opportunity costs of his own labour and the use of his capital. His true profit is calculated as follows.

Revenue	£s	Costs	£s
Gross income	22 000	Materials, lighting,	
		heating, transport, etc.	9 000
		'Labour'	8 500
		Interest foregone	600
			18 100
		Profit	3 900
	22 000		22 000

81 a (i) Firm A, £10 000; Firm B, £20 000.
(ii) Firm A, 50 per cent; Firm B, 40 per cent.
b (i) Firm B (ii) Firm A

82 It would have no effect since the revenue and marginal cost curves remain unchanged.

83 (*a*) It tends to discourage the taking of risks, especially those associated with the introduction of new products, new techniques, and ventures into new markets.
(*b*) Reduces the funds available for private investment.
(*c*) Distorts the absolute differentials in the prospective returns from low-risk and high-risk projects.

Multiple choice questions

84 C

85 D $[\dfrac{15p}{xp} = \dfrac{10}{100}$, therefore, $x = 150p]$

86 C

True or false?

87 a True

b False   [The tax falls on the surplus remaining *after* all costs have been met; only normal profits are regarded as a cost of production.]

c False

d True   [Opportunity costs include imputed costs (e.g. costs of entrepreneur's own labour) as well as paid-out costs.]

Data response questions

88 The 20 per cent dividend obviously bears some relation to the economist's idea of normal profits, and the profit in excess of this amount is what we regard in economic theory as abnormal profit. The reference to surplus profit implies that it is regarded as a form of economic rent. The distribution of profits to workers is much closer to modern thinking (and practice) than to classical ideas on profits. It is now widely recognised that those who contribute labour to production are also risk-bearers – they risk unemployment if the enterprise fails. An important motive in profit-sharing schemes is the idea that when a worker stands to benefit financially from the success of a firm he will become much more closely identified with management's objectives and the traditional worker–management antagonism will diminish or disappear.

89 a The Iranian revolution led to some reduction of oil supplies on the world market and to fears that the situation would further deteriorate and lead to even more severe restrictions of supply in the future. The effect was a sharp increase in the price of oil. The windfall gains to oil producers represented a form of economic rent since the price of oil greatly exceeded the reward necessary to persuade the producers to remain in the business of producing oil.

b It would probably have little effect since the tax would be levied on that part of the producers' income which took the form of economic rent. Only if the tax reduced profits below the level of normal profit (for this industry) would there be any serious effects on price and output.

Answers to part 7

1 Money

Short answer questions

1 (*a*), (*b*), and (*d*).

2 Acceptability, portability, durability, divisibility, and limited in supply.

3 The development of a note issue with a fractional backing of gold. The goldsmith-bankers began to issue notes of greater total monetary value than the gold held in their strongrooms. They were, therefore, able to create money and make loans.

4 A company is bankrupt when its liabilities exceed the current value of its assets. The banks referred to here were not insolvent in this sense. The value of their assets covered their liabilities, but these assets were not sufficiently liquid to meet their depositors' demands for cash when there was a loss of confidence in the banks.

5 Bank deposits are created by the commercial banks and the backing for this part of the money supply takes the form of various types of securities (i.e. the banks' claims on the wealth of borrowers).

6 No. Banks do create money in the form of bank deposits. They do, however, also exchange a liquid asset (money) for illiquid assets (claims on the property of the borrowers).

7 a Its liquidity and the certainty of its *money* value.
b It earns no income and its exchange value may fall.

8 In making a loan, the bank credits the account of the borrower but there is no corresponding or balancing reduction in other bank deposits.

9 It assumes that *V* and *T* are constant.

10 $D = 1/r \times LA$

11 The relationship is *V* (the velocity of circulation of money) because total expenditure = supply of money × *V*.

Multiple choice questions

12 C **13** B **14** C

15 C [The £10 million cash deposit will support bank deposits of £100 million. The payment of the cash into the bank will create a deposit of £10 million so that the banking system will be able to create a further £90 million of deposits by making loans.]

16 B.

True or false?

17 a False **b** True
  c False [Wealth consists of *real* assets; money represents claims to wealth.]
  d False
  e True [If people wish to hold money equal in value to $\frac{1}{5}$ of the annual value of transactions, then each unit of money must, on average, change hands 5 times each year ($V = 5$). If they decide to hold money equal to $\frac{1}{4}$ the annual value of transactions then V will be 4.]
  f True.

Data response question

18 Many interpretations are possible.

There is some degree of exaggeration in the charges levied against the various groups and professions mentioned. In recent years, especially through the medium of television, there have been some commendable efforts to help the general public understand some of the mysteries of medicine, technology and finance. The people engaged in these fields have generally displayed a willingness to cooperate in these activities.

Nevertheless, for most people, a veil of mystery covers the operations of financial institutions. To some extent this is due to the fact that there is no visible or tangible product and no clearly visible production process. We cannot *see* what is happening. The people in the world of finance are dealing with money, but this money is merely some figures on computer tapes. The 'creation' of this money differs from the creation of most of the other things we use in our daily lives because it comes into being by processes which are commonly associated with the *recording* of things rather than the *making* of things. Most of our money is created by mere bookkeeping exercises. It is the nature of modern money which is responsible for the mystique which surrounds it rather than any conspiracy by modern bankers to delude the general public.

The most practical and useful definition of money is that it is whatever is generally acceptable in exchange for goods and services. In other words, 'money is what money does'. Notes and coin are obviously money; not so obvious perhaps is the fact that bank deposits are money. But these are a fairly logical development from notes and coin. Just as claims to gold (notes) superseded gold, so claims to notes and coins (bank deposits) have become more important than the notes and coin.

2 The banking mechanism

Short answer questions

19 The government's banker; the bankers' banker; the lender of last resort; the agent responsible for managing the national debt; the central note-issuing authority for the UK; the Treasury's agent in the foreign-exchange market; the operator of the government's monetary policy.

20 Banknotes represent claims against the issuing bank. Originally these claims were claims to gold (the notes were convertible). Since the Issue Department has no obligation to convert its notes to gold, its 'liability' amounts to no more than an obligation to replace an old banknote with a new one.

21 **a** Discounting refers to the act of purchasing a security for less than its nominal or redemption value.
b Base rate is the rate of interest which the joint stock banks charge on their loans to the most credit-worthy borrowers (e.g. local authorities and nationalised industries).
c 'Accepting' refers to the act of endorsing a bill of exchange so as to guarantee payment on the bill should the drawee default.

22 Cash ratio deposits are those deposits which all banks above a certain size must hold at the Bank of England. The deposits are non-interest-bearing and in 1984 amounted to $\frac{1}{2}$ per cent of a bank's eligible liabilities.
Operational deposits are the clearing banks' working balances held in current accounts at the Bank of England.

23 Banks have obligations to their shareholders to make adequate profits and obligations to their depositors to maintain an adequate supply of liquid assets. The most liquid assets, however, are the least profitable while the most illiquid assets are the most profitable.

24 They usually call in their money market loans.

25 No. Banks cannot lend unless there is a demand for loans from credit-worthy borrowers. In times of depression there may be very little demand for loans even at very low rates of interest. Also they cannot lend unless they can persuade people to deposit money with them.

26 Heavy sales of the banks' investments (securities) would lead to a fall in their market values and involve the banks in substantial capital losses. A liquid asset is one which can readily be converted into cash with little risk of capital losses.

27 Large banks are better able to withstand financial crises. With a large number of depositors, no single depositor can embarrass the bank by withdrawing his funds. With many branches, large banks have a geographical spread of risks enabling them to withstand slumps in any one region. Larger organisations generally command more confidence than smaller ones – this is important in banking. In recent years large banks have been able to make use of large expensive units of capital (computers, data-processing machines) where the average costs of operation fall quite rapidly when capital costs are spread over a large number of accounts.

28 Interest is charged on the full amount of a bank loan whether the loan is fully spent or not. With an overdraft, interest is only charged to the extent that the account is overdrawn. An overdraft allows a firm much greater flexibility in arranging its financial commitments.

29 Bankers can easily convert some of their liquid assets into cash, but this would still leave the total of liquid assets below its former level. If a bank's supply of liquid assets falls below the prudent operational ratio, its lending activities will be restricted.

30 The discount houses.

31 In the inter-bank market, banks borrow and lend large sums of money between themselves. The market serves to smooth out short-term variations in the liquidity positions of different banks.

32 In view of the increased importance of open market operations in the conduct of monetary policy, the Bank of England, in 1981, took steps to ensure that the discount houses had sufficient funds to maintain an active market in bills of exchange and Treasury bills.

33 A Euro-dollar deposit refers to a deposit denominated in dollars which is placed with a financial institution located outside the USA. For example, if the owner of a dollar deposit with an American bank transferred the title to that deposit to a London bank, he would have a dollar claim on the London bank, and the London bank would have a dollar claim on, say, a New York bank.

34 Private sector sterling time deposits. (NB public sector sterling deposits were included in £M3 until February 1984.)

Multiple choice questions

35 A 36 C 37 C 38 D 39 B.

40 A [Statement 1 means that the bankers' balances at the central bank will be reduced.]

41 C 42 B 43 B 44 D.

Data response question

45 a *Liabilities*

Public deposits: the government's main accounts.

Special deposits: 'frozen assets' of the commercial banks. Payments are made into these accounts when the central bank wishes to reduce the liquidity of the banking system.

Bankers' deposits: See answer to question 22, page 178.

Reserves: retained profits.

Other accounts: accounts of overseas central banks, international institutions and some private customers.

Capital: a vestigial item from the days when the Bank was a joint stock company.

Assets

Government securities: bonds, Treasury bills and temporary loans to the National Loans Fund.

Advances: loans to the money market.

Other securities: any other securities of whatever kind including market purchases of commercial bills.

Notes and coin: held for issue to the commercial banks

b (i) Notes and coin £7 m. − £1 m. = £6 m. Bankers' deposits (operational) £199 m. − £1 m. = £198 m.

(ii) Special deposits £711 m. − £100 m. = £611 m. Bankers' deposits (operational) £199 m. + £100 m. = £299 m.

(iii) Government securities £1150 m. − £50 m. = £1100 m. Bankers' deposits (operational) £199 m. − £50 m. = £149 m.

3 Monetary policy

Short answer questions

46 a Payments are made to the government's account at the Bank of England by cheques drawn on the commercial banks. When these cheques are cleared, the bankers' balances at the Bank of England are reduced and this constitutes a loss of cash to the commercial banks.

b When government payments are made by means of cheques drawn on the Bank of England, the clearing of the cheques will increase the bankers' balances at the Bank of England. These transactions will increase the banks' cash reserves.

47 The expression refers to the situation when the commercial banks, through shortages of cash, are obliged to call in their money-market loans. In order to meet their obligations to the commercial banks, the discount houses will be obliged to borrow from the Bank of England.

48 In order to influence or control the level of expenditure in the economy, the monetary authorities try to control particular monetary variables. These variables are the targets of monetary policy. There is a variety of possible targets, the main ones being the stock of money, the rate of interest, bank credit, and the rate of exchange.

The instruments of monetary policy are the tools or techniques which the central bank uses in order to influence the targets of monetary policy. In recent years the UK monetary authorities have made use of the following instruments: open market operations, direct controls, reserve requirements, funding, and the central bank's lending rate.

49 If the supply of money is fully determined by the monetary authorities, then, like any other monopolist, they can determine either the quantity *or* the price (i.e. the rate of interest). They cannot determine both.

50 In a slump when prices are falling, an interest rate of 5 per cent may prove a formidable deterrent to borrowers – there may be very few opportunities for profitable investment. In the middle of an inflationary boom when prices are rising rapidly, a nominal interest rate of 10 per cent will represent a very low (or even negative) real rate of interest.

51 (*a*) An information lag – it takes time to collect and process the relevant data.

(*b*) An implementation lag – due to the problems associated with discussing alternatives and agreeing on appropriate policies.

(*c*) A reaction lag – the lag in the response of the target variables to changes in the intermediate variables. For example, a change in interest rates will not bring about immediate changes in spending and saving. It takes time for households and firms to revise their saving and investment plans.

(*d*) A lag between a change in demand and a change in supply – changes in production take time.

52 a Penal borrowing refers to loans obtained from the central bank when its lending rate is higher than the rate of interest in the open market.

b By using open market operations to produce a situation where the commercial banks are short of cash. This obliges them to call in money-market loans and the discount houses will be forced to borrow from the central bank.

c The discount houses.

d Money-market rates of interest will not be allowed to fall much below the central bank's lending rate because of the costs of borrowing at this penal rate. The discount houses will try to minimise these costs by keeping their own lending rates close to the central bank's lending rate.

53 a When the balance of payments is in deficit it may be necessary to stem (or reverse) the flow of short-term capital out of the country. This may be achieved by raising the rate of interest, but this will increase the costs of the government's borrowings.

b While an increase in the rate of interest may be successful in improving an adverse balance of payments situation, it may inhibit the government's attempts to increase aggregate demand if the economy is moving into a recession. A higher rate of interest may discourage investment and, by increasing the exchange rate, make exports more expensive.

54 The Bank of England determines short-term rates of interest through the buying and selling of bills, that is, by open-market operations in the money market.

55 An obligation was placed on all banks having eligible liabilities of £10 million or over to hold a sum of money equal to $\frac{1}{2}$ per cent of their eligible liabilities in the form of non-interest-bearing balances at the Bank of England. These banks are also obliged to keep a minimum amount in loans to the members of the London Discount Market Association.

56 'Fine-tuning' refers to attempts to operate short-term controls on the economic system. Monetarists argue that because of the inadequacy of the present state of knowledge about the working of the economic system and because of the existence of various lags (see answer to question **51**), discretionary monetary policy is more likely to be a de-stabilising rather than a stabilising influence.

Multiple choice questions

57 A

58 B [The tax payments will cause a movement of funds from the bankers' balances at the central bank to the Exchequer.]

59 D **60** B

61 B [The increased demand for pounds will cause sterling to appreciate thus raising export prices in overseas markets.]

True or false?

62 a False **b** False **c** True **d** True **e** False

f False [The working balances are the operational deposits.]

g True [The increased supply of government securities will tend to lower their prices and hence raise interest rates.]

Data response questions

63 a A great deal of productive activity is financed with borrowed funds. A firm may not be able to begin (or expand) production unless it can obtain working capital (or, to an increasing extent, medium-term capital) from the banks.

b The granting of a bank loan is dependent on the banker's assessment of the borrower's ability to repay. The loan creates a liability for the bank (in the form of a deposit) and this is balanced on the other side of the balance sheet by the bank's claim on the borrower. The value of this asset therefore depends on the quality of the banker's judgement.

c (*a*) The purchase of stocks and shares for speculative purposes.

(*b*) The purchase of land and property for speculative purposes.

(*c*) The purchase of commodities in the futures market.

d The property boom in 1972/3 led to much criticism of the banks because bank loans had played a large part in the speculation in property. These events indicated that some degree of control over the quality of bank advances might be needed. The problem is, however, who is best qualified to judge whether the bank loan is for a 'desirable' proposition and whether the borrower has the ability to use the funds efficiently. The commercial banker's knowledge of the day-to-day operations in the world of industry and commerce is probably much more extensive than that of the monetary authorities.

To some extent controls on the direction of bank advances are already applied. When bank lending has been restricted by tight monetary policy, the authorities have advised banks on how they should apply the restraints (e.g. no restrictions on loans to help exporters and firms in development areas; severe restrictions on loans for consumption and speculation).

One may query the validity of the last sentence of this quotation. A loan to finance production is also speculative – the product may not sell. It does not automatically follow that 'a banker who finances production can be repaid out of production'.

64 a Funding refers to the sale of longer-term government securities on the open market. The purchasers of these securities will pay for them with cheques drawn on accounts in the commercial banks and the clearing of these cheques will reduce the bankers' balances at the Bank of England. The reduction in the banking system's liquidity will restrict its lending activities.

b Other things being equal, increased sales of securities will tend to lower their market prices. A fall in the market price of fixed-interest securities means that the market rate of interest (the yield) increases. In this particular case, the demand for gilt-edged securities was very strong and the increased supplies of securities were absorbed without any downward pressure on security prices. In fact, excess demand raised security prices so that yields actually fell.

c This means that the monetary authorities made no attempt to influence the conditions in the money market which brought about the fall in short-term interest rates. In other words, they did not use open-market operations to offset the influence of market forces.

Answers to part 8

Short answer questions

1 When prices change in the ratio 100:125, the value of money changes in the ratio 125:100. The value of money, therefore, would fall by 20 per cent.

2 The proportions of total expenditure devoted to different commodities as revealed by the Family Expenditure Surveys.

3 It will rise by 1.0 per cent.

4 Price index for year 2 = 103.

5 (*a*) When the additional money is absorbed into idle balances (i.e. when *V* falls);
(*b*) When supply is elastic (i.e. some resources are unemployed) so that additional spending can be matched by increased output.

6 The exchange value of wealth held in the form of money declines during inflation. A hedge is a means of protecting property and the term is used in the financial world to describe a means of protecting the exchange value of wealth by holding it in the form of assets whose exchange values do not fall during inflation.

7 A budget deficit; an export surplus; an increase in investment not matched by an increase in savings (or taxation); an increase in spending financed by an increase in the money supply.

8 This refers to the difficulties which governments have encountered when trying to maintain full employment *and* stable prices. Many economists believe that the two objectives are incompatible. The evidence for these views derives from studies (e.g. the Phillips curve) which showed that, over many years, the annual rate of change of prices was inversely related to the levels of unemployment. On the basis of this evidence it appeared that governments were faced with the unpleasant choice of higher rates of inflation *or* higher levels of unemployment – they could 'trade off' one objective against the other. In more recent years, however, many countries have experienced rising levels of unemployment *and* increasing rates of inflation.

9 Assume (*a*) wages account for 70 per cent of total costs, (*b*) any increase in wages is fully passed on in the form of higher prices, (*c*) any increase in prices is always fully matched by an increase in wages which restores real wages to their former level.

If prices increase by 10 per cent, wages will also increase by 10 per cent. This will raise costs and hence prices by 10 per cent of 70 per cent = 7 per cent. Wages will now increase by 7 per cent causing costs and prices to rise by 7 per cent of 70 per cent = 4.9 per cent, and so it will go on. The rate of inflation is diminishing.

10 (*a*) An increase in indirect taxes;

(*b*) an increase in import prices (this may be due to an increase in world demand, a fall in world supplies, or a depreciation of the currency).

11 a Costs are inflexible downwards. Wages make up the greater part of total costs and even when unemployment levels are relatively high, unions have shown strong resistance to any attempt to cut money wages. Some costs are beyond the control of producers (e.g. imported materials) while others are often fixed on a long-term contractual basis (e.g. fixed interest loans, insurance premiums, rents, etc.). Larger organisations will resist the temptation to indulge in price wars (see textbooks on oligopoly).

b The inevitable result is falling output and falling employment.

12 a The annual rate of change of wage rates compared with the rate of unemployment. Since there is a close correlation between the movements in wages and the movements in prices, the Phillips curve is often used to show the relationship between the rate of inflation and the level of unemployment.

b The Phillips curve was based on statistical evidence which showed that over many years (up to the mid-1960s) price stability was associated with an unemployment rate of about $2\frac{1}{2}$ per cent. In recent years, however, high rates of inflation have been associated with high levels of unemployment (e.g. in 1975 prices rose by 24 per cent while unemployment averaged 4 per cent).

If (ii) is a correct explanation, it means that any given level of unemployment is now associated with a much higher rate of inflation than that portrayed in the original Phillips curve. Among the many explanations for the shift of the curve are:

A much more militant attitude by unions whose bargaining positions are not so susceptible to higher unemployment rates as they used to be.

The economy has been increasingly affected by cost-push pressures which are not related to domestic wage pressures (e.g. higher import prices).

Learning to live with inflation has escalated wage demands.

Increasing dissatisfaction with relatively slow growth of real incomes has also led to an escalation of wage demands.

13 (*a*) A steady increase in the general price level,

(*b*) a relatively high level of unemployment, and

(*c*) a zero or negative rate of economic growth.

14 Other things being equal, an increase in the general price level would lead to a fall in the quantities of goods and services demanded and hence to lower outputs and higher levels of unemployment. Governments anxious to avoid the unemployment consequences of higher prices will be tempted to 'finance' higher incomes by allowing the money supply to increase. This will mean that quantities demanded and, hence, employment will not fall, at least, in the short run.

15 The most common measure of excess demand has been the relationship between the number unemployed and the number of unfilled vacancies. The degree of excess supply may be measured by expressing unemployment as a percentage of employment. Alternatively the number of unfilled vacancies might be used as an indicator of excess demand, but the figures for vacancies are not so complete as those for unemployment. In recent years, however, these measures of excess demand (or excess supply) have become much less reliable because a given level of vacancies is now associated with much higher levels of unemployment than it used to be. The reasons are complex, but it is suggested that

(a) a greater percentage of those out of work are now registering themselves as unemployed,

(b) unemployed workers now spend longer looking for new jobs,

(c) employers who previously 'hoarded' labour during a recession, in the expectation that it would be short-lived, have adjusted to the idea that demand–management techniques will not be used to reduce unemployment and have ceased to hoard labour.

16 The natural rate of unemployment is that which, given the existing structure of the labour market, equates the demand for and supply of labour; it is the rate which is consistent with a stable rate of inflation. The rate of inflation will be stable when the expected rate is equal to the actual rate.

An increase in aggregate demand will tend to raise money wages and this will be interpreted as an increase in real wages. If the rate of productivity is constant, however, the increased demand and the higher wage rates will raise prices and real wages will fall back to their former level. The temporary increase in 'real' wages will tempt more workers into the labour force, but this increase in employment will be temporary; as real wages fall back to their former level, employment will fall. Some workers attracted into employment by the 'illusion' of higher real wages will leave the labour force.

Multiple choice questions

17 D **18** D **19** C **20** A **21** B **22** C
23 C

[Commodity	Weighted index (year 2)
A	$2 \times 150 = 300$
B	$3 \times 80 = 240$
C	$5 \times 120 = 600$
	$10 \div 1140$
	$= 114$]

24 B [Increasing wage rates are not inflationary if they are accompanied by increasing productivity.]

25 C

True or false?

26 a True **b** False **c** True **d** False **e** True **f** False

Data response question

27 a Yes. Cost-push inflation is shown as originating either in the labour markets or through higher import prices. Excess demand is shown as working through the labour markets (i.e. excess demand for labour bids up wage rates and these higher costs are passed on as higher prices).

b The common factor is the wage–price spiral. It can arise from a labour shortage or via cost-push pressures. Increased prices, whatever the originating factors, will set up a wage–price spiral which will keep the inflationary process going.

c Once inflation has been experienced for a few years a 'price-increase' and 'wage-increase' psychology develops. In economic theories which deal with the workings of the capitalist system we often come across the term 'self-fulfilling expectations'. When people expect something to happen and adjust their behaviour in the light of these expectations, the actions they take often *cause* the very events they have been anticipating. This may well be an important element in the inflationary process. When people expect inflation to continue, it *will* continue, because unions press for wage increases to compensate for anticipated price increases and firms try to adjust prices to anticipate cost increases. There is a tendency for inflation to accelerate as people revise their expectations of inflation upwards. They try to avoid a fall in the value of their money by moving out of money into goods, and firms and unions will raise prices and wages by the amounts that they anticipate others will be raising theirs, quite independently of the state of demand.

Answers to part 9

1 International trade

Short answer questions

1 a Country B **b** 'less'

2 a Country A **b** Country B **c** (ii)

3 No, because the opportunity costs of producing food and clothing are the same in both countries.

4 Britain has (or had?) a comparative advantage in the production of manufactured goods. The output from factors of production employed in manufacturing will exchange for a greater quantity of food in world markets than the factors could have produced had they been employed in British agriculture.

5 2 units of food.

6 800 units of food: 250 units of clothing, i.e. 16F:5C.

7 (a) [The trading possibility line begins at the output which represents 100 per cent specialisation on clothing.]

8 a Exports 125 units of clothing. **b** Imports 400 units of food.

9 (a) A country might have a potential cost advantage in the development of a certain industry, but because of an earlier start, this industry has been developed in another country and it is now so large and well established that it would be impossible for a small new industry to compete with it on the basis of free trade. In this situation a tariff might be necessary to allow a new industry to grow in a country where it has a potential comparative advantage.
(b) Tariffs were (are?) held to be necessary to protect those industries (e.g. steel, chemicals, agriculture) which produce the essential needs when a nation is at war.

10 A specific tariff is based on the quantity imported. Thus a tariff of, say £1 per pair on imported footwear would be a relatively small charge on expensive footwear but a relatively large tax on cheap footwear.

11 If a nation indulges in a high degree of specialisation, it becomes very vulnerable to changes in demand and to technical innovations.

12 (*a*) Tariffs raise domestic prices while subsidies tend to lower them.

(*b*) Tariffs raise revenue for the government but subsidies mean an increase in government expenditures.

(*c*) It depends on the nature of the product, but tariffs, being an indirect tax, may act regressively (placing a relatively larger burden on the poor), whereas if subsidies are financed from progressive taxes, they can reduce the inequality of income.

13 It refers to favourable *price* movements. It means that export prices have risen relative to import prices, so that any given volume of exports now exchanges for a larger volume of imports.

14 (*a*) Import prices rising faster than export prices;

(*b*) export prices falling faster than import prices;

(*c*) export prices falling, import prices stable;

(*d*) import prices rising, export prices stable;

(*e*) export prices falling, import prices rising.

15 If the demand for exports is elastic, total foreign currency earnings will increase (assuming supply of exports is elastic).

If the demand for imports is not perfectly inelastic (i.e. elasticity of demand > 0), foreign currency expenditures on imports will fall.

Multiple choice questions

16 A

17 C   [If the tariff is truly prohibitive, it will yield little or no revenue.]

18 B   [A quota, by reducing supply, will raise prices in the home market. Both quotas and tariffs can be applied to particular goods (i.e. used selectively).]

19 C

20 D   [The fact that country B produces more of both goods does not indicate that it has an absolute advantage because we have no information on the *input* of resources.]

21 C   [See comments on answer to question **20**.]

True or false?

22 **a** True   **b** False   **c** False   [Labour costs depend upon wage rates *and* productivity; very inefficient low-wage labour will be high-cost labour.]
d False   [Because the opportunity cost ratios would be the same in both countries.]   **e** False   **f** True

Data response questions

23 a See Figure 41. (i) $0Q$ (ii) QQ_1 (iii) $0Q_1$
  b (i) $0Q_2$ (ii) Q_2Q_3 (iii) $0Q_3$ (iv) $PP_1 \times Q_2Q_3$
  c The tariff has (a) benefited home producers since domestic output and employment have increased; (b) enabled the government to obtain revenue (but this is merely a transfer from consumers to government); (c) harmed world producers, since their total income from this market has fallen from $QQ_1 \times 0P$ to $Q_2Q_3 \times 0P$; (d) adversely affected home consumers, since they now consume less and pay higher prices.

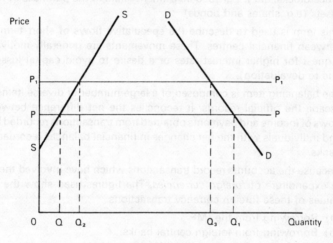

Figure 41

24 a The term *structural adjustment* refers to the movement of resources from one industry to another. When a country loses a comparative advantage in a particular industry, the demand for the product of that industry will fall both at home and abroad. There will be pressures for the home market to be protected and, if this policy is adopted, other nations might retaliate. Developments such as these diminish international trade. The full benefits of greater specialisation and trade can only be obtained if resources are mobile and able to move from industries which are losing their comparative advantage to those which have the ability to develop a comparative advantage.
  b International debts must be serviced (i.e. interest paid on them) and repaid in foreign currency. In the longer run these foreign currencies must be earned by selling goods and services overseas.
  c The removal of restrictions on international trade would mean lower prices for producers and consumers. The greater specialisation and competition encouraged by freer trade would lead to lower-cost production.

2 International payments and the rate of exchange

Short answer questions

25 **a** Visible trade **b** Capital account **c** Invisible trade **d** Invisible trade **e** Invisible trade **f** Invisible trade **g** Capital account **h** Official financing

26 Real investment refers to the purchases of real assets (factories, mines, office blocks, etc.). Portfolio investment refers to the purchase of financial assets (e.g. shares and bonds).

27 This term is used to describe the speculative flows of short-term capital between financial centres. These movements are generally motivated by a quest for higher interest rates or a desire to avoid capital losses (e.g. due to devaluation).

28 The balancing item is composed of a large number of diverse items which escape the official records. It reconciles the net difference between the flows of income and payments obtained from transactions recorded by firms and individuals with the net changes in financial balances recorded by the banks.

29 Because the accounts record transactions which have involved the receipt or expenditure of *foreign currencies*. The figures used show the sterling values of these foreign currency transactions.

30 (*a*) Borrowing from the IMF.
   (*b*) Borrowing from foreign central banks.
   (*c*) Withdrawals from the official foreign currency reserves.

31 **a** +30 **b** +90 **c** −65

32 A capital outflow reduces the foreign currency reserves and enters the balance of payments as a debit item. In future years, however, this invest-ment will yield an income (i.e. interest and profits) in the form of foreign currency. This inflow of foreign currency appears as a credit item in the balance of payments.

33 The faster pace of technical progress and modernisation in some mature industrialised countries and the emergence of newly industrialised countries eliminated Britain's comparative advantage in some manufacturing in-dustries while she continued to be a substantial importer of foodstuffs and raw materials. In the late 1970s and early 1980s this situation changed when Britain became a major oil producer but there remained a substantial deficit on *non-oil* visible trade.

34 One country's surplus is another country's deficit. If some countries run persistent surpluses then deficit countries may have to resort to import controls with the result that all countries will be adversely affected by the consequent reduction in world trade. A balance-of-payments surplus represents an injection into the circular flow of income and could be a contributory cause of demand-pull inflation.

35 By using some kind of weighted average of the changes in the rates at which the currency is exchanging against a number of major currencies (this calculation is now known as the effective exchange rate index).

36 'Convertible'

37 (a) Stability and certainty – unexpected and frequent changes in the exchange rate create uncertainty and discourage the flow of trade. For example, under a floating-rate system a British buyer of American cotton may have a price quoted in dollars, but his costs are uncertain because the dollar–pound exchange rate may change between the date of the contract and the date when payment falls due. (NB A forward market reduces this uncertainty.)

(b) A bulwark against inflation – where domestic inflation causes a balance of payments deficit the country will be losing foreign currency reserves and this will force the government to take steps to deal with the inflation.

(c) Encourages economic integration – note, for example, the great difficulties which have arisen, as a result of floating rates, in implementing the EEC's policy of common farm prices.

38 Resources are not perfectly mobile so that supplies of different goods and services cannot be quickly adjusted to the changes in relative prices as the exchange rate changes. Floating exchange rates tend to encourage speculation and this might have a destabilising influence on the balance of payments. In the case of a deficit, the resulting fall in the exchange rate (making imports dearer) could lead to cost-push inflation and to further falls in the exchange rate.

39 A deficit implies that, in the foreign exchange market, the supply of the currency will exceed the demand for it at the current rate of exchange and its external value will tend to fall. To maintain the fixed rate, the authorities must *buy* the domestic currency (i.e. increase the demand for it) and for this purpose they will use their supplies of foreign currency; the reserves will fall.

40 a (b) and (c) **b** (a)

41 Profits can be made by the following sequences of exchanges:
(a) francs for pounds, pounds for dollars, dollars for francs;
(b) dollars for francs, francs for pounds, and pounds for dollars.
There transactions will change the supply and demand conditions until the exchange rates are in line. This activity is known as *arbitrage*.

42 If the debt is expressed in terms of foreign currency, the real burden increases. It now requires a greater volume of exports to earn the foreign currency required to make the interest payments (and capital repayments).

43 Devaluation has an immediate effect on relative prices – but the volumes of exports and imports change more slowly. In spite of the increased home prices of imports, the volumes are not likely to change much in the short period (there will be contractual arrangements and alternative sources of supply will take time to develop). Export prices fall, but it will take time to expand the volume. Hence the immediate effect of devaluation is a fall in export earnings while expenditures on imports (in foreign currency) stay much the same. The balance of payments deficit probably gets worse! In time, however, supplies adjust to changes in price and quantities demanded. Export earnings increase and imports are reduced, or grow more slowly. The balance of payments situation improves. A gradual worsening followed by a marked improvement = J effect.

44 Example: if money-market rates in London are higher than those in other financial centres, short-term funds will be attracted to London and the inflow of foreign currencies will improve the UK balance of payments (and raise the demand for pounds on the foreign exchange market).

45 (*a*), (*b*), and (*c*).

Multiple choice questions

46 A   **47** C   **48** C   **49** D   **50** E   **51** C

True or false?

52 a False   **b** True   **c** True   **d** True   **e** False
f True   ['Hedging' in this context refers to financial transactions which aim to reduce the risk of capital losses due to changes in the exchange rate.]
g False   [When a country is on a fixed exchange rate, an increase in the foreign currency prices of imports means a corresponding increase in terms of the home currency.]

Data response questions

53 The fall in exports has been more than offset by measures to restrict imports. These may have taken the form of tariffs and quotas, or deflationary measures such as higher taxes and increased interest rates while reductions in the money supply may also have been used to reduce home demand. In year 1 the country was financing long-term investment overseas (60) largely with short-term borrowings (40) which can be quickly withdrawn (at the expense of the reserves). Lack of confidence clearly reversed this flow of short-term funds in year 2 and the outflow may well have been stemmed only at the cost of much higher domestic interest rates (see answer to question **44**). The fall in long-term investment abroad was probably due to the imposition of controls on the availability of foreign currencies for this purpose. The 'improvement' in the basic balance masks a recession and illustrates the point that the existence or absence of a balance-of-payments deficit is no guide as to the existence or absence of a balance-of-payments problem.

54 a Real exchange rates take account of the different rates of inflation in different countries. The nominal exchange rate is adjusted for differential inflation between trading partners.

b Under a system of fixed exchange rates, changes of parity take the form of devaluation or revaluation. The current economic situation of a country gives speculators a fairly clear idea of which way the parity will be moved. A country with a persistent deficit is almost certain to devalue its currency. A speculator who sells a currency before devaluation and buys it back after devaluation makes a profit on the transaction.

c Central banks spend foreign currency when they intervene in the foreign exchange market to support their currencies (see answer to question **39**). In recent years central banks have cooperated in supplying funds for this purpose so as to offset downward pressures on currencies which were due to speculative pressures and to exceptional hot-money flows.

3 International cooperation

Short answer questions

55 To promote and make provision for the following: international monetary cooperation; exchange stability and avoidance of competitive exchange depreciation; full convertibility of currencies; assistance to enable countries to overcome balance-of-payments difficulties so that they do not have to resort to trade restrictions; to ensure that growth of world liquidity is sufficient to meet growth of trade.

56 They 'purchase' foreign currencies from the Fund – using their own currencies for this purpose.

57 It refers to the fixed exchange rate system (more precisely, the adjustable peg system) which was adopted at Bretton Woods. Certainty is regarded as the great advantage of fixed exchange rates.

58 Borrowings from certain member countries (mainly the advanced industrialised countries and the OPEC countries). These will provide, on request from the IMF, and subject to certain conditions, supplementary supplies of foreign currencies.

59 a Those assets which are generally acceptable in settlement of international indebtedness.

b Gold, convertible national currencies, borrowing facilities (e.g. at IMF), international reserve assets (e.g. SDRs). (SDR = Special Drawing Rights.)

c Countries maintain reserves of internationally acceptable liquid assets: (*a*) as working balances to finance trading transactions; (*b*) to deal with temporary balance-of-payments deficits; (*c*) to use in foreign-exchange markets when they wish to 'manage' the exchange rate; (*d*) to meet net withdrawals by overseas holders of short-term funds.

A very uneven distribution of world liquidity (e.g. in relation to each country's share of world trade) may mean that countries short of reserves may be forced to impose trade restrictions when they experience deficits. In theory the need to hold reserves is much reduced when exchange rates are floating.

60 SDRs are internationally acceptable liquid assets created by the IMF. They are allocated to each member country in amounts according to its quota and they can be used to buy the currencies of any other member for the purposes of settling imbalances in international payments. The value of an SDR is expressed as a weighted average of a number of major currencies.

61 Countries forming free-trade areas do not enter into any commitment other than an agreement for the mutual elimination of quotas, tariffs, and other trade barriers. Customs unions are more closely knit and in addition to the abolition of trade barriers between members they have a common tariff on imports from non-member countries. Customs unions or common markets usually provide for the free movement of factors of production within the area and aim for a high degree of integration of the separate economies.

62 The advantages claimed for these groupings are:
(*a*) Greater scope for the operation of the principle of comparative advantage – resources will shift from the relatively high-cost producers to the relatively low-cost producers.
(*b*) More scope for industries to obtain economies of scale.
(*c*) Greater competition will lead to increased efficiency.
(*d*) A further advantage stemming from (*b*) is that industries within the area will be able to compete more effectively in world markets.

63 European farmers are protected from competition from lower-cost world producers by a system of import levies on foodstuffs. A Guarantee Fund exists to maintain farm prices at agreed levels. When prices tend to fall below these levels the Fund intervenes by making purchases to maintain minimum prices and stockpiles its purchases. To maintain European production it can also subsidise exports of foodstuffs. A Guidance Fund also exists to help finance the restructuring of European agriculture (e.g. to encourage the integration of small farms).

64 The major item of expenditure is the Guarantee Fund which supports farm prices.

65 The Council of Ministers consists of one minister from each member country. It takes all the major decisions about Community policy. Ministers directly represent their national governments.

The Commission is responsible for the day-to-day operations of the Community. It carries out policies decided by the Council of Ministers. The Commissioners are drawn from different member countries but they represent the Community as a whole and act independently of their own national governments.

66 (a) Subsidies to home producers;

(b) state-owned enterprises giving preference to home producers when ordering equipment;

(c) drafting safety regulations, technical specifications, and design requirements which deliberately favour home producers;

(d) collusion between producers in different countries (e.g. price, output, and marketing agreements designed to restrict competition).

67 a The IMF provides short-term assistance to governments to enable them to overcome balance-of-payments difficulties.

The World Bank grants long-term loans designed to foster economic development.

b The IMF obtains most of its funds from the subscriptions of member governments (it can also borrow on short term from some of these governments).

The World Bank also has capital subscribed by member countries but obtains most of its funds by selling long-term securities on the world's capital markets. It can also guarantee loans raised by member countries.

68 Loans and grants provided by governments; loans and grants provided by international institutions. Some authorities also regard private investment (e.g. by multinational companies) as a form of aid. Other forms of aid consist of gifts, or the provision, on favourable terms, of consumer goods (e.g. food); technical assistance (e.g. services of architects, engineers, economists); education facilities (scholarships for students from LDCs); trade (preferential treatment for exports from LDCs, long-term commodity agreements).

69 LDCs experience a low level of income, therefore saving is low, therefore ability to invest is low, therefore economic growth is low, therefore income is low.

70 (a) If a tariff is levied then it should apply at the same rate on imports from all members of GATT.

(b) A member that reduces its tariffs on imports from another country should in return obtain a comparable concession on its exports.

71 (a) Costly to initiate scheme – large funds required to finance purchases;

(b) costly to operate (i.e. storage, handling, insurance, and interest charges);

(c) difficult to estimate minimum price (i.e. price at which fund will buy stocks), and maximum price (i.e. price at which stocks will be sold). For example, if minimum price is fixed too high, managers of buffer stock could find themselves building up huge stocks and exhausting their funds.

Multiple choice questions

72 B   **73** C   **74** D   **75** A

True or false?

76 a True   **b** True   **c** True   **d** False   **e** True

Data response question

77 a Trade diversion occurs in the case of commodity X. Before the formation of the union, country B (low-cost producer) exports X to country A. After formation of the union, country C exports X to country A. Production has been shifted from low-cost to high-cost producer.
b Trade creation occurs in the case of commodity Y. Before union, country A does not import Y but after formation of customs union it imports Y from country C. Resources will be re-allocated towards the lower-cost producer.

Answers to part 10

Short answer questions

1 a The Consolidated Fund and the National Loans Fund.

b The Consolidated Fund handles the government's revenue (mainly taxation) and meets its expenditures on goods and services (including support grants for local authority services, the health service, and so on).

The National Loans Fund handles the government's domestic lending and borrowing.

2 (*a*) Law and order, defence, public administration, coastguard services, etc.

(*b*) Factory inspection, Town and Country Planning, Regulation of companies (The Companies' Acts), Control of Monopolies and Restrictive Practices, etc.

(*c*) Control of industrial location, subsidies to key industries, investment grants, state ownership of industry, various state agencies to promote restructuring of industry, grants for research and development.

(*d*) Use of taxation and welfare benefits to redistribute income and wealth; promotion of greater equality by state provision of health and education services, etc.

(*e*) Use of Budget deficits and surpluses to expand the economy or to curb inflationary tendencies. Government may also use its control of the money supply and the exchange rate for similar purposes.

3 The central government, local authorities, nationalised industries, and other public corporations.

4 About 60 per cent of public spending represents a direct claim on output. It is spent in buying goods and services (e.g. wages to teachers, policemen, and doctors) and on equipment for schools, hospitals, the armed forces, power stations, etc. The other 40 per cent is handed back to households and firms as transfer payments in the form of social security payments, investment grants, interest on the national debt, etc.

5 Once the rates of certain social security benefits have been set, the total expenditure on these items is not directly controlled by the government. For example, an increase in the numbers unemployed automatically leads to more public expenditure on the appropriate social security benefits.

6 Income tax, corporation tax, petroleum revenue tax, VAT, and the excise duties on oil, tobacco, and alcoholic beverages.

7 National insurance contributions.

8 a Official holdings: The National Debt Commissioners, government departments, and the Bank of England.
Financial institutions: banks, insurance companies, building societies, etc.
Individuals and private trusts.
Overseas residents.
b Long-term government securities; Treasury bills; National Savings Certificates and Premium Bonds; loans by overseas financial institutions.

9 Since most of the debt carries a fixed rate of interest, inflation has greatly reduced the interest 'burden' in real terms.
Over most of the post-war period the national debt has grown more slowly than GDP.

10 If the proportion of elderly dependents is increasing and the real value of state pensions is maintained (by means of indexation), the burden, in the form of taxation, of state aid to the elderly will increase.

11 a Proportional **b** Regressive **c** Progressive

12 Equality of sacrifice might be taken to mean that different income groups should suffer the same loss of utility. If income is subject to the law of diminishing marginal utility, then equality of sacrifice would seem to require that *proportionately more* of the higher incomes should be taken in taxation.

13 (*a*) Unemployment benefits, child allowances, pensions;
(*b*) health and education services;
(*c*) subsidies on housing, school meals, and foodstuffs.

14 a It describes who actually pays the tax in terms of reduced income or higher prices.
b (i) The person on whom the tax is levied,
(ii) producers and/or consumers – the proportionate shares depend on the elasticities of demand and supply.

15 The Public Sector Borrowing Requirement (PSBR) represents the extent to which the public sector as a whole borrows from other sectors of the economy. The Central Government's Borrowing Requirement (CGBR) represents the government's own borrowing but the funds it borrows are much greater than it requires for its own purposes since some of the money borrowed is re-loaned to other parts of the public sector (e.g. local authorities and public corporations).

16 a An increasing PSBR will mean an increased demand for loans (i.e. an increased supply of securities). The price of securities will tend to fall and the rate of interest will tend to rise.
b Other things being equal, if part of the increase in the PSBR is financed by borrowing from the banking system, there will be some increase in the money supply.

17 The 'poverty trap' relates to a variety of social security benefits which are intended to help the low-income families. These families qualify for benefits such as the family income supplement, rent and rate rebates, free milk, and free school meals. It is possible that a relatively modest increase in income might raise the income of such a family above the level which qualifies it for the receipt of these particular benefits. Thus, with a rising income, a poor family faces not only a rising tax bill (including National Insurance contributions) but the loss of certain benefits, so that it might well find itself with a lower net real income.

Multiple choice questions

18 C   **19** A   **20** D   **21** A   **22** A   **23** C   **24** A

True or false?

25 a True   [When demand is inelastic, a subsidy will have a relatively large effect on price.]
b False   **c** True
d True   [The increase in government borrowing will increase the supply of securities. The prices of these securities will tend to fall and market rates of interest will tend to increase.]
e True   **f** True

Data response questions

26 a See Figures 42 and 43.
b Marginal tax rates are an important influence on incentives since they determine the net rewards for harder or more efficient work. Average tax rates measure the proportion of total income taken in tax and demonstrate how the burden of the overall level of taxation is distributed. Scheme A sets out to be far more progressive than scheme B and has much higher marginal rates of tax. It would, therefore, tend to have a greater effect on incentives although this can be exaggerated because the effect depends upon how many people actually pay these higher rates. Scheme B might have less effect on incentives because no matter how much people earned the tax authorities would never take more than 35 per cent of their extra income.
In spite of the marked difference in the structure of the taxes, Figure 43 shows that they are almost equally progressive and hence would have similar effects on the distribution of income.

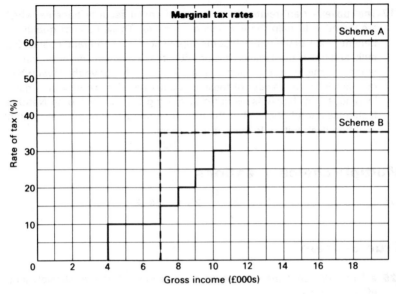

Figure 42

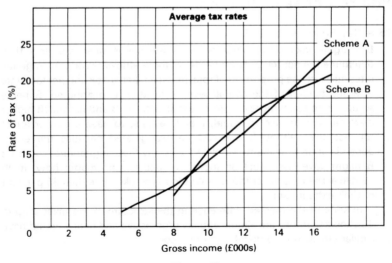

Figure 43

27 a Changes in the general price level and changes in total expenditure will both have effects on government revenue from taxation. Some taxes such as VAT, capital gains tax, and stamp duties are directly related to prices.

The effect of an increase in the general price level depends upon the cause of the price increase. If it is due to an increase in demand, revenues from indirect taxes will increase. If it is due to cost increase, the effect on tax revenue will depend upon the price elasticities of demand of the commodities subject to taxation.

Changes in expenditure will directly affect tax revenues. If expenditure increases because real income has increased, tax revenues will be influenced by the income elasticity of demand of the commodities subject to taxation.

b Income-earners receive tax-free allowances before they start paying income tax. For example, in the UK, in 1984, the personal allowance was £2005 per annum and the married man's allowance was £3155 per annum. The value of these allowances is usually adjusted each year to take account of the effects of inflation. In other words, these allowances are indexed. Tax thresholds refer to the starting points of the different bands of taxable income. Each band of income is taxed at a different rate (see question **26**). As with personal and other allowances, tax thresholds are usually adjusted to allow for the effects of inflation.

c The fact that the projected rise in oil prices has not produced an estimated increase in tax revenue from North Sea oil is due to the fact that output from the North Sea is expected to fall after 1985.

Answers to part 11

1 The economy as a whole

Short answer questions

1 From firms to households: (*a*) a flow of payments for factor services, (*b*) a flow of goods and services.
From households to firms: (*a*) a flow of factor services, (*b*) a flow of payments for goods and services.

2 A leakage is any income which is not passed on within the circular flow. An injection is any addition to the income of domestic (i.e. not foreign) firms that does not arise from the spending of domestic households or any addition to households' income which does not arise from the spending of domestic firms.

3 MPC decreases, MPS increases

4 MPC = 0.5 **5** APC = 45/40 = 1.125

6 Saving = 5 **7** Equilibrium level of income = 90.

8 a Saving is defined as that part of income which is not spent on consumption goods and services. Investment is defined as that part of output which is not consumed.

b Unplanned investment consists of unanticipated additions to stocks arising from an excess of supply over demand.
Realised investment = planned investment + unplanned investment
$$= \quad 20 \quad + \quad 10$$
$$= 30$$

9 Initially total savings will increase, but the increase in APS will reduce *C* so that income will fall. It will continue to fall until total saving returns to its former level. Income will return to an equilibrium level where planned saving equals planned investment (which has not changed). APS will increase but the equilibrium level of total saving will remain unchanged.

10 a Multiplier = 1/(1 − MPC) = 5

b Increase in income = £10 000 + £8000 + £6400 + £5120 + ...
Increase in saving = £2000 + £1600 + £1280 + £1024 + ...

c Eventual increase in income = 5 × £10 000 = £50 000

11 a Leakages = taxation + saving + imports.

b Injections = government spending on goods and services + investment + exports.

12 a 'leakage'

b Multiplier $= \dfrac{1}{\text{mps} + \text{mpm} + \text{mrt}}$

(where mps = marginal propensity to save, mpm = marginal propensity to import, and mrt = marginal rate of taxation).

13 Multiplier $= \dfrac{1}{\text{mps} + \text{mpm} + \text{mrt}}$

$= \dfrac{1}{0.15 + 0.1 + 0.2}$

$= 2.2$

14 $Y = C + I + G + X - M$; $\quad I + G + X = S + T + M$

15 In equilibrium, $\qquad I + \quad G \quad + X \quad = \quad S + \quad T \quad + M$

$\qquad\qquad\qquad\qquad$ £70m. + £80m. + £50m. = £80m. + £90m. + M

Missing item is imports which must be equal to £30m. in order to establish equilibrium.

16 ab is a deflationary gap.

17 a ab   **b** EF/ab.

18 a It is stable and predictable.

b If the rate of growth of the money supply is strictly controlled, the rate of growth of money national income will be controlled. If labour presses for and succeeds in obtaining wage increases which exceed the growth of productivity, costs and prices will increase. The inevitable consequence will be a fall in the quantities of goods and services demanded; output and employment will fall.

19 The supply of many commodities may be inelastic in the short run so that increased demand will tend to raise prices.

Organised labour may take the measures to increase demand as a 'green light' for improved wage settlements and strong unions will probably succeed in raising wages faster than productivity. The increase in aggregate demand will tend to make it easier for employers to submit to demands for higher wages so that costs and prices will increase.

Multiple choice questions

20 C   [Since MPC = 0.6, the multiplier = $1/(1 - 0.6) = 2.5$]

21 B   **22** E   **23** C

24 B   [$Y_d = 0.8Y$, therefore, $S = 0.25Y_d = 0.25 \times 0.8Y = 0.2Y$]

25 A

26 C   [The fall in spending will have a downward multiplier effect. Income might fall to an extent which causes total saving to fall even though APS has increased.]

True or false?

27 a False
b False   [The output of goods and services *is* the national income. Equilibrium requires that planned spending = planned output.]
c False   **d** True   **e** False
f True   [Equilibrium requires that *total* leakages = *total* injections.]
g True   [This is another way of saying that the larger the MPC, the larger the multiplier.]
h True

Data response question

28 a Disposable income = total factor income *minus* direct taxes *plus* transfer payments.
b In equilibrium, $Y = C + I$
$$Y = 0.75Y + £1000m.$$
$$Y = £4000m.$$
c Disposable income = $0.8Y$
$$C = 0.75 \times 0.8Y = 0.6Y$$
$$S = 0.25 \times 0.8Y = 0.2Y$$
(i)   Multiplier $= \dfrac{1}{mps + mrt}$

$$= \dfrac{1}{0.2 + 0.2}$$

$$= 2.5$$
(ii) In equilibrium, $Y = C + I$
$$Y = 0.6Y + £1000m.$$
$$Y = £2500m.$$
d In equilibrium, $Y = C + I + G$
$$Y = 0.6Y + £1000m. + £1000m.$$
$$Y = £5000m.$$

2 Economic policies

A Full employment

Short answer questions

29 No, because stability of employment as well as the level of employment is an objective of policy. Instability adds to uncertainty and diminishes economic welfare.

30 a Multiplier = $1/(1 - \text{MPC}) = 1/(0.25) = 4$
In order to raise income by £10 000 million, therefore, it will be necessary to raise aggregate demand by £2500 million.
b Increases in aggregate demand tended to (*a*) lead to balance of payments deficits because of the UK's high propensity to import and (*b*) raise costs and prices because of immobilities and increased pressures for higher wages.

31 A progressive income tax; unemployment payments and supplementary benefits; a progressive rate of National Insurance contributions; a system of deficiency payments (e.g. to farmers).

32 It will tend to raise the demands for the products of the growth industries (those that are already short of labour). The effect will be to raise the prices of the products of, and the wages in, these industries.

33 A government has the ability to increase aggregate demand but the distribution of this demand is largely determined by consumers. Changes in the pattern of consumer spending must be matched by corresponding movements of resources if full employment is to be maintained, and the danger of inflation due to 'bottlenecks' is to be avoided.

34 (*a*) Costs of unemployment and supplementary benefits,
(*b*) loss of income tax and national insurance contributions, and
(*c*) lower receipts from indirect taxation.

35 Two main reasons: (*a*) the size of the working population increased, and (*b*) productivity increased faster than total output.

36 Investment grants are particularly attractive to capital-intensive industries. A substantial grant to a firm in these industries may, therefore, create relatively few jobs.

37 The natural rate of unemployment is regarded as an equilibrium rate in the sense that it is consistent with a *stable* rate of inflation (not necessarily a zero rate).

Multiple choice questions

38 D **39** A **40** B **41** B **42** E

True or false?

43 a False **b** True **c** False **d** False

Data response question

44 (*a*) Rising real disposable income: as real incomes rise people tend to spend a greater proportion of income on personal, financial, and leisure services.

(*b*) Increasing real incomes in other countries have contributed to an increased foreign demand for UK services (e.g. airlines, hotels, restaurants).

(*c*) A lower income elasticity of demand for manufactured goods than for services.

(*d*) Manufacturing sells more of its output overseas and is subject to a greater degree of competition.

(*e*) Demographic changes: for example, the increased proportion of elderly people has led to an increased demand for medical services.

(*f*) Changes in technology: for example, the growth in computer services.

(*g*) Increasing competition from foreign suppliers of manufactured goods to the UK.

B Inflation

Short answer questions

45 It is *realised saving* and *realised investment* which are always equal. In a two-sector economy excess demand will arise when planned investment is greater than planned saving at the current level of income.

Saving makes investment possible, it does not cause investment to take place. A reduction in the rate of interest will tend to *increase* investment. A large part of total saving is not very sensitive to changes in the rate of interest.

46 a The *real* rate of interest may still be relatively low.

b If it reduces investment, the rate of economic growth in the immediate future will be adversely affected.

47 (*a*) An increase in the velocity of circulation,
(*b*) the widespread adoption of money substitutes (e.g. letters of credit, credit cards (e.g. Access, Barclaycard), etc.).

48 a An increase in import prices; an increase in indirect taxes; wages rising faster than productivity where wages are pushed upwards by trade union pressures rather than bid upwards because of labour shortages.
b See Part 8, question **27** and the answers to parts **b** and **c** on page 188.

49 a 'Thinner profit margins' indicates that intensified competition has obliged producers to absorb some of the cost increases instead of passing them on in the form of higher prices.
A rising pound means that the sterling prices of imports are falling.
b 'Thinner profit margins' will tend to discourage investment and reduce the flow of funds available for investment.
A rising pound will increase the foreign currency prices of British exports and tend to restrict the growth of exporting industries.

50 The deflationary effects arose because of the adverse movement of the terms of trade of the oil-importing countries and because the demand for oil is very inelastic. The inability of some major oil exporters to spend the huge increase in their foreign currency earnings in world markets meant that there was a large withdrawal from the international circular flow of income. The oil importers' expenditures on oil rose very sharply and this constituted a much greater leakage from their economies. The effect was similar to a government imposing a large increase in taxation without any increase in its own spending.
The inflationary effects were due to cost-push pressures arising from the very large increases in oil prices.

51 a 'money supply'.
b 'Excessive wage claims means wage claims which called for an increase in wage rates much greater than the increase in productivity.

52 a During inflation the opportunity cost of holding money balances is the fall in the exchange value of money (as compared with wealth held in assets whose real value does not fall). This cost is offset to some extent if the money is held in a time deposit on which interest is paid. When the rate of inflation falls, the opportunity cost of holding a current account balance (a sight deposit) falls and may be outweighed by the greater convenience of sight deposits.
b M1 includes sight deposits but not time deposits and the lower rate of inflation encouraged some transfer of funds from time deposits to sight deposits.

53 Price controls prevent the price mechanism from carrying out its function of allocating resources. Changes in supply and demand cannot fully reveal themselves in the form of price changes, and surpluses and shortages will not be eliminated by price adjustments. All prices cannot be controlled and they will rise very sharply in the uncontrolled sectors. Black markets will develop in the sectors subject to price control. Equitable distribution of goods subject to price control requires some form of physical rationing. To what extent these are 'disadvantages' is a value judgement. The main criticism of price controls is that they do not deal with the causes of inflation but only with its symptoms. They might, however, encourage the acceptance of wage restraint.

54 a To reduce the rate of inflation.

b If an incomes policy succeeds in restricting the rate of growth of money incomes to the rate of growth of output, the upward pressures of costs on prices will be eliminated. In other words, prices will not be increased by movements of supply curves to the left.

Since demand is determined largely by income, a successful incomes policy should also ensure that demand does not increase faster than supply at current price levels.

Multiple choice questions

55 C

56 B   [Subsidies on goods with inelastic demands would cause a significant decrease in total spending on these goods. This would increase consumers' ability to buy other products, the demands for which would increase.]

57 A   **58** A

True or false?

59 a False

b False   [Even if $G = T$, excess demand will occur if $(I + X) > (S + M)$.]

c False   [Taxation is a leakage from the circular flow so that an increase in taxation will have deflationary effects. Reactions to the tax increases might cause inflation.]

d True

e False   [An increase in the *general* price level means that aggregate income also increases.]

f True

Data response question

60 a When inflation is fully anticipated, all contracts will have the actual rate of inflation built into them. Nominal interest rates will include a return which fully compensates for inflation and wage contracts and the tax system will be fully adjusted to the actual rate of inflation.

b (i) The tax system in most countries was not designed for inflationary conditions. Direct taxes are usually levied on nominal incomes and the allowances and thresholds are also usually based on nominal incomes. Where this is the case, rising nominal incomes will pull people into higher tax brackets although, due to inflation, their real incomes may not have increased at all.

(ii) Inflation reduces the real value of government debt and the costs of servicing the debt.

(iii) Where the rate of inflation increases because the government is financing part of its borrowing by means of an increase in the money supply, inflation acts as a form of taxation. In effect, the government is increasing its own purchasing power by reducing the purchasing power of other sectors of the economy.

C   The balance of payments

Short answer questions

61 EEC, GATT, IMF.

62 a It will need an adequate supply of foreign currencies to enable it to intervene in the foreign exchange market. When the value of its currency is tending to fall the central bank will use its reserves of foreign currencies to buy its own currency. (See also Part 9, question **39**, and answer on page 193.)

b From the IMF and foreign central banks.

63 'One country's imports are another country's exports' – a sharp fall in the imports of a major trading nation will reduce incomes in the exporting countries and this, in turn, will reduce the ability of these countries to absorb imports.

64 It will require a relatively large fall in aggregate demand to bring about a significant decrease in imports. In other words, there would be a serious effect on the level of employment.

65 a lower   **b** raise.

66 a *Exports* – foreign prices fall 5 per cent, volume increases 10 per cent, therefore foreign currency earnings increase to $10000 × 95 per cent × 110 per cent = $10450.

Imports – sterling prices increase 5 per cent, volume falls 5 per cent, but dollar prices remain unchanged, therefore foreign currency expenditures fall to $11000 × 95 per cent = $10450.

b Increased demand from abroad would tend to raise domestic prices and potential gains from devaluation might not be fully realised.

c It would probably deflate (i.e. reduce) home demand, thus releasing some home supplies for export markets.

67 (a), (b), and (c).

68 **a** Its direct effect on employment is relatively small because the production of gas and oil are capital-intensive activities.

b Government revenues from North Sea oil are very substantial (about £10 billion in 1984–5). In the 1980s these revenues increased quite rapidly because of (a) increasing output from the North Sea, and (b) the fact that oil companies' costs of exploration and development are allowed in full against taxation and by the mid-1980s most of these allowances had been used up.

c North Sea oil has had a significant impact on the UK's balance-of-payments. The likely balance-of-payments benefit for 1985 was estimated to be £10 billion. The major effect, of course, has been on visible trade where the UK has moved from being a large-scale importer of oil to a net exporter (1981). The favourable effect on visible trade is offset to some extent by the increased flow of interest profits and dividends abroad (much of the investment in the North Sea was by foreign oil companies).

69 Effective exchange rates are a way of measuring a currency's external value in a manner similar to that used to measure changes in its internal value (i.e. by means of a price index). The effective exchange rate of sterling is calculated as a weighted average of its rates of exchange against the currencies of several other countries (chosen so as to reflect their importance as trading competitors).

Multiple choice questions

70 D

71 B [The General Arrangement to Borrow (GAB) is an agreement to supplement the resources of the IMF.]

72 C **73** B

True or false?

74 **a** True

b True [For example, other countries can only increase their dollar balances if the USA runs a balance-of-payments deficit; this allows other countries to acquire claims on the USA.]

c False **d** False **e** False **f** False

Data response question

75 a Speculators believed that wealth held in the form of some other currencies was subject to risks of (i) capital losses due to anticipated depreciation or devaluation, or (ii) a loss of liquidity due to the expected imposition of exchange controls, or (iii) confiscation, where there was a high degree of political instability.

b In recent years (early 1980s) the governments of both the UK and USA have operated strict controls on the rate of growth of the money supply as a major feature of their anti-inflationary policies. To this end, high interest rates have been used as an instrument to reduce the demand for bank loans. But high interest rates attracted foreign funds to the UK and USA and, by increasing the demands for pounds and dollars, tended to raise their external values.

c When a currency is overvalued, it means that its external value in terms of other currencies is greater than the value which is obtained by comparing its purchasing power (in terms of goods and services) with the purchasing power of other currencies. It means that the exports of a country whose currency is overvalued are relatively expensive and its imports are relatively cheap, hence the demands for restrictions on imports.

D Economic growth

Short answer questions

76 a The movement from A to B represents an increase in national output arising from a greater use of existing capacity (i.e. putting unemployed resources to work). The movement from B to C represents an increase in the productive capacity of the economy.

b Both are described as economic growth although many economists restrict the usage of the term to describe an increase in productive capacity.

77 Changes in real national income per head.

78 As an economy grows, workers press for shorter hours and longer holidays; the proportion of the population in the labour force tends to decline as more younger people stay on into further education, and people retire earlier.

79 (*a*) There is an almost universal demand for higher standards of living.

(*b*) Growth makes it easier to carry out policies of income redistribution – inequalities can be reduced without having to reduce anyone's income.

(*c*) Increased social expenditures can be undertaken without any increase in tax rates.

(*d*) Costs of defence are much easier to bear.

(*e*) Much political prestige now attached to growth rates.

80 Slightly less than 3 per cent per annum (2.9 per cent approximately).

81 The same growth rates applied to different bases will yield different absolute increments in total output. For example, 3 per cent of £100 million is a much larger sum than 3 per cent of £10 million. A further reason for the widening gap in living standards is the much higher rate of population growth in developing countries.

82 Capital-widening occurs when the capital stock is increased proportionately to the increase in the supply of the other factors of production – the ratio of capital per worker remains unchanged. Capital-deepening takes place when the ratio of capital to the amounts of other factors is increased – each worker has more capital to work with.

83 Technical progress; the rate of investment; the quality of investment; improvements in education and technical training; economies of scale; reallocation of resources from low-growth to high-growth industries.

84 They may find the social costs of growth unacceptable; they may object to the necessary sacrifice of higher levels of consumption in the *immediate* future as more resources are devoted to investment.

85 a In attempting to speed up the rate of economic growth, governments have tried to stimulate investment and output by increasing aggregate demand. Under conditions of full employment, however, the necessary movement of resources from consumer goods' industries to capital goods' industries requires an increase in saving and/or taxation if a situation of excess demand is to be avoided. On some occasions the increase in withdrawals was not sufficient to prevent inflation.
Due to immobilities the supply of some goods and services is inelastic and increases in demand tended to create inflationary pressures. An increase in aggregate demand also led unions to raise their wage demands so that increased spending led to higher prices rather than higher outputs.
b As industry attempts to increase output it will increase its imports of raw materials and capital equipment. Higher incomes will also lead to increased imports of consumer goods and services. In the early stages of economic growth, imports tend to increase faster than exports.

86 Not necessarily. While the rate of investment is an important determinant of economic growth, there seems to be no close correlation between the two. Nations with the same rates of investment have achieved very different growth rates. Much depends upon the type of investment, the quality of investment, and the efficiency with which the new capital is utilised.

Multiple choice questions

87 E **88** C **89** B

True or false?

90 a True **b** False **c** True **d** True **e** True **f** True

Data response question

91 a These are innovations which provide a great stimulus to private investment both in the new industry and many related industries (e.g. railways in the nineteenth century). The great impetus given to investment has large multiplier effects throughout the economy.

b Most developing countries have balance-of-payments problems due to their heavy dependence on imported manufactured goods of all kinds, and to the fact that their export earnings, due to the instability of commodity prices, tend to be very volatile. The difficulties of earning enough foreign currency to finance the most essential imports make any development programme which has a low import content very attractive to developing countries.

c It is a labour-intensive industry – the bulk of the income goes to labour in the form of wages – workers will have large MPCs – hence large multiplier effect.

d Strategy lays emphasis on self-reliance; the programme can be implemented across the entire country; demand for housing and other buildings is virtually limitless; the programme could well stimulate new forms of credit and financing and it should help to mobilise savings.

E Inequalities of income and wealth

Short answer questions

92 Great inequalities in ownership of land (main source of income); the rich often have great political power and can resist movements towards reform of land ownership; no effective system of taxation and public expenditures to carry out transfers of income and wealth; new enterprises often capital-intensive and benefit the rich more than the poor.

93 Earnings from employment are the main source of total personal income and these earnings are more equally distributed than the investment income provided by personal wealth; there is no lower limit to possible ownership of assets but there is a lower limit to income; there is no inherent limit to amount of wealth a person can own but the earning capacities of individuals are limited; wealth can be inherited but earning capacity cannot.

94 The rates of estate duty (i.e. death duty) rose sharply during this period and this may have led to some redistribution of wealth in order to avoid the higher tax rates. There has been a large increase in home ownership and a sharp increase in house prices. The *real* value of shares has tended to decline.

95 Previous estimates of the distribution of personal wealth only took account of marketable assets and money holdings. The Royal Commission thought that such things as accumulated pension rights should be counted as personal wealth.

96 (*a*) Inheritance, capital gains, gambling winnings, savings and investment.
(*b*) They believe that saving and investment should be encouraged because these are essential to economic development.

97 a While income tax is progressive, indirect taxes act regressively. If government revenue were to be raised solely by direct taxes, the rates would be extremely high, even on average incomes, and there would be serious disincentive effects.
b Social security benefits are very progressive, as are subsidies on foodstuffs.

98 People tend to move up the earnings ladder as they grow older. Many of those in the bottom half of the distribution in, say, 1978, will be in the top half in 1998.

99 These flat-rate or universal benefits make a much larger proportionate contribution to the real income of poorer families.

100 a By assuming that the law of diminishing marginal utility applies to income and that everyone derives the same satisfaction from a given amount of income.
b Incomes are also incentives to production. It seems necessary to offer higher rewards to encourage people to work more efficiently, accept greater responsibility, undertake longer training, develop new ideas, and so on.

101 Land, houses, shares, government securities, insurance policies, works of art, personal possessions (cars, furniture, jewellery), bank deposits, cash.

102 The capital transfer tax falls on *additions* to wealth – it takes effect when the ownership of wealth is transferred. A wealth tax falls (annually) on the *accumulations* of wealth and is potentially a more powerful instrument for achieving a more equal distribution of wealth.

103 a It is a positively skewed distribution. This is true of all income distributions in all countries. Most people have an income which is below the average because the relatively small numbers with very high incomes pull the average to a higher value than the mode (i.e. the most frequently occurring, or 'typical' income).
Differences in earnings arise from differences in natural ability, length of education and training (not everyone has equal access to the educational and training sectors), length of work experience, restrictions

on mobility by unions and professional bodies, amount of responsibility carried, motivation, and to some extent, luck.

b Improvements in the opportunities for, and quality of education; reform of out-of-date training systems; removal of institutional and social barriers to mobility.

F   Public ownership and control

Short answer questions

104 The electricity industry is the sole (UK) buyer of specialised generating plant, heavy cables, etc.; British Telecom is the sole buyer of certain types of telecommunications equipment; British Rail is the sole buyer of certain types of rolling stock and other railway equipment; and the NCB is the only domestic customer for some types of coal-cutting equipment.

105 *Shareholder*: the ownership of a nationalised industry is vested in the state which is, in effect, the sole shareholder.

Banker: the government is responsible for raising the funds required by these industries, either by direct provision or as guarantor when the money is raised elsewhere.

Paymaster: the government has overall responsibility for the financial position of the nationalised industries and must ultimately cover any losses they may incur.

106 Faced with rising costs and unable to raise their prices, the nationalised industries make huge losses. These must be covered by government subsidies financed by higher taxation or increased government borrowing (which could raise interest rates), or by reduced government spending on other projects.

107 They may be covered by cross subsidisation, that is, profitable services subsidise the unprofitable services, but the government has accepted responsibility for some loss-making services and provides a subsidy to cover the deficit in revenues.

108 As monopolists, many nationalised industries have sufficient market power to raise prices so as to make abnormal profits. On the other hand they may be making losses simply because the government is forcing them to hold down their prices.

109 *British Rail*: cheap fares on off-peak services.

British Telecom: lower rates for off-peak telephone calls.

Electricity Boards: lower tariffs for off-peak electricity, industrial tariffs lower than domestic tariffs.

110 Industries where the technical conditions of production are such that competition would lead to a wasteful use of resources (e.g. duplication of fixed capital) and where there are important economies of scale which can only be fully realised by a sole supplier. Examples are the supply of such products and services as water, electricity, gas, telephone communications, and railway transport.

111 Information on such matters as (*a*) movements in productivity, (*b*) quality of services, e.g. British Rail – extent to which the trains run on time; Post Office – average time taken to deliver a letter; British Telecom – availability of direct dialling, and so on.

112 Public control of an industry's marketing policies, prices, and dividends; acquiring shares in companies and putting government representatives on the management boards; taking the wholesale stage into public ownership; public supervision and control of the technical specifications of the product.

Multiple choice questions

113 C

114 D [FFI stands for Finance for Industry, a finance corporation which exists to provide funds for industry.]

115 A [EDC stands for Economic Development Committees which operate within the framework of the National Economic Development Council. They study the problems of particular industries and propose measures to increase industrial efficiency.]

116 A

Data response question

117 a (i) Increasing returns.
(ii) Capital-intensive industries where the optimum size of plant is very large.

 b (i) If this guideline is to be followed, then price must cover average cost. In Figure 37 price will be equal to 0P and output equal to 0Q.
(ii) This guideline indicates that a policy of marginal cost pricing should be adopted in which case price will be $0P_1$ and output $0Q_1$. There are considerable difficulties in applying this principle, a major one being the problem of estimating marginal cost. Furthermore, a nationalised industry which is obliged to take account of externalities should fix price equal to marginal social cost, and it is extremely difficult to attribute a money value to externalities.

It is clear from Figure 37 that the nationalised industry cannot satisfy *both* conditions. Marginal cost pricing would mean that the industry makes losses (price < average cost).

A compromise solution is often adopted in the form of a two-part tariff (e.g. electricity, gas, and telephone prices) where the consumer pays a standing charge as a contribution to fixed costs and a variable charge directly related to his or her consumption of the commodity.